LIVING ENGLISH GRAMMAR AND COMPOSITION

M.L. TICKOO, M.A. (Lond.), PH.D. (Lond.)
A.E. SUBRAMANIAN, M.A., L.T. (Madras)
P. R. SUBRAMANIAM, M.A., L.T. (Madras)

Orient BlackSwan

LIVING ENGLISH GRAMMAR & COMPOSITION

ORIENT BLACKSWAN PRIVATE LIMITED

Registered Office
3-6-752 Himayatnagar, Hyderabad 500 029 (A.P.), India
e-mail: centraloffice@orientblackswan.com

Other Offices
Bangalore, Bhopal, Bhubaneshwar, Chennai, Ernakulam, Guwahati, Hyderabad, Jaipur, Kolkata, Lucknow, Mumbai, New Delhi, Patna

First published by Orient Longman Pvt. Ltd., 1983
Reprinted 1984, 1986, 1991, 1993, 1997, 1998, 2003, 2004, 2006
First Orient Blackswan impression 2010

ISBN 13: 978 81 250 1032 6
ISBN 10: 81 250 1032 7

Printed in India at
Aadi Printech
Delhi

Published by
Orient Blackswan Private Limited
1/24 Asaf Ali Road
New Delhi 110 002
e-mail: delhi@orientblackswan.com

PREFACE

The first part of this book is a presentation of the key-points in the structure of English grammar. As such, it aims to answer a fully-defined set of linguistic needs and is recommended for the learner who has a foundation of the essential components.

In preparing this book, special attention has been given to strengthening "weak" areas of knowledge. Care and thought have also gone into framing a grammar textbook which, while exhaustive and comprehensive, also takes into account the number of teaching hours generally available at the university level for the teaching of grammar. The book has been divided into units to facilitate teaching within the given time.

The book covers, in suitable depth and detail, items commonly covered at this level. In doing so it does not, however, lose sight of an important characteristic of current English—that certain aspects of its structure can be better learned as parts of larger topics than in isolation.

The composition section has been divided into four chapters. Each chapter gives guidance in the skills that are involved and each provides specimen materials, hints and suggestions suited to the intermediate learner. Each one also sets tasks for the learner. In setting these tasks we have, on the one hand, stayed away from themes that are much too abstract or far too removed from his experience and, on the other, attempted to provide enough challenge to stimulate his interest and attention and make him strive for his best.

It is our hope that the book will go a long way in giving the learner valuable insights into the system and structure of modern English and in putting him on his feet in written English.

M.L. Tickoo
A.E. Subramanian
P.R. Subramaniam

CONTENTS

GRAMMAR

COMPOSITION

1 THE NOUN PHRASE

Subject	Predicate
Birds	fly.
Sarojini Naidu	was a great poet.
A bicycle	has two wheels.
My watch	has been stolen.
That man	is my neighbour.
Some boys	were playing in the garden.
The cold	was unbearable last winter.

Each of the subjects above is a noun with or without another wo, before it.

A noun with or without a determiner (a, my, that, some, the, etc. is called a **noun phrase**. It can occur in the subject part or predicate part. The noun is the key or 'head' word in a noun phrase.

Nouns

Nouns are of three kinds:

i. *Proper nouns*: Kamala, Hamid, Ravi, Delhi, India, The Ganga, The Alps, etc.

ii. *Countable nouns*: Countable nouns can be singular: a book, my bicycle, that hill. In every case we put one of the determiners before it.

Countable nouns can be plural.

Cows eat grass.
My *books* have been stolen.

Forms of Genders

1 Some nouns add /ess/ to form their feminine gender. If the noun ends in /e/, it drops the /e/ before adding /ess/. Sometimes there is a change in spelling.

god — goddess   prince — princess
waiter — waitress   emperor — empress

2 A few nouns indicate the gender by the prefix *he* or *she*:

he–goat she–goat he–wolf she–wolf

3 Some nouns take special endings:

hero–heroine viceroy–vicereine

4 A number of nouns occur in pairs, one noun referring to the male class, and the other to the female.

bachelor	—	maid	uncle	—	aunt
brother	—	sister	father	—	mother

5 Some nouns are common to both the male and female members of the class:

cousin child cook doctor

6 Note the feminine genders of the compound nouns given below:

son-in-law	daughter-in-law
men teachers	women teachers
grandfather	grandmother

iii. *Uncountable nouns*

1 Uncountable nouns fall into the following groups:

a. Things considered in mass: rice, wheat, hair, dust, etc.
b. Materials: paper, wood, cloth, gold, etc.
c. Liquids: water, milk, oil, etc.
d. Gases: air, hydrogen, smoke, etc.
e. Natural phenomena: heat, cold, electricity, sunlight, etc.
f. Abstract nouns: courage, friendship, freedom, happiness (some of these are countable: sorrow, punishment.)
g. Branches of learning: Mathematics, Economics.

2 There are some uncountable nouns we refer to by their parts. We use them with expressions such as *a piece of*, *a kilo of*, etc.

Plurals: pieces of chalk, flashes of lightning,
drops of water, slices of bread, etc.

Determiners

Below is a group of words used before nouns to fix or define them in some way or other. They are called determiners.

1 Demonstratives: *this, that, those, these.*
2 Possessives: *my, your, his, her, its, our, their.*
3 *some, any.*
4 Articles: *a, an, the.*

When *some* is used with a countable noun in the plural, it means an unknown or indefinite number.

Some persons were hurt in the accident.
Some articles have been stolen from the house.

When *some* is used with an uncountable noun, it means an indefinite quantity.

I would like to buy a notebook and some paper.
He brought a pen and some ink.

Any is rarely used in affirmative sentences. It is generally used only in negative and interrogative sentences.

There isn't any sugar in the house.
I have some bread, but I haven't any biscuits.
Is there any milk in the jug?

Exercise 1

Fill in the blanks with *some* or *any*.

1 There are ______ history books written in Hindi in the library. There aren't ______ geography books.
2 We saw ______ boys there; we didn't see ______ girls.
3 There aren't ______ hippos in the zoo; there are ______ rhinos.
4 The tourists visited ______ temples; they didn't visit ______ other places of interest.
5 I don't want to eat ______ more rice. I would like to have ______ more bananas.

The Genitive

Mr. Kurup's sons go to school.
Kurup's is the genitive form of *Kurup*.
The roof of the house was blown off in the cyclone.
Of the house is the genitive of *house*.

	Example	Form
a	the boy's bag James's children	/'s/ is added to singular nouns.
b	children's toys men's clothes	/'s/ is added to plural nouns not ending in /s/.
c	birds' nests boys' school	Only /'/ is added to plural nouns ending in /s/.
d	Jesus' parables Moses' laws	Only /'/ is added to singular nouns with two or more /s/ sounds.

e	goodness' sake conscience' sake	Only /'/ is added when *sake* follows a noun ending in /s/ sound.
f	King of Nepal's palace	/'s/ is added to the last noun in the case of a phrase with two or more nouns.
g	Alexander the Great's conquests Moti the carpenter's shop	/'s/ is added to the second noun when there are two in apposition.

Choice of the /'s/ genitive

/'s/ genitive is used in the case of animate nouns, especially persons. In the case of inanimate objects /of/ genitive is used. /'s/ genitive is also used in phrases such as *a year's delay, a nation's morale*, etc.

In these expressions we have both the /'s/ genitive and the /of/ genitive:

a friend of my father's — one of my father's friends
a book of Keats's — one of Keats's books

Exercise 2

Put together the following pairs of nouns using the *'s* genitive or the *of* genitive:

Pratap, car; house, window; Gandhiji, statue;
a day, work; a month, holiday; the picture, the frame;
my father, properties; the girls, school;
a day, wages; India, frontiers;
cow, milk; conference, venue;
elephant, memory.

2 ARTICLES

The words ***a, an,*** and *the* are called *Articles*; ***a*** and ***an*** are called *indefinite* articles and *the* is called the *definite* article. *A* is used when the sound following it is a consonant: a book, a uniform. *An* is used when the sound following it is a vowel: an elephant, an hour.

Some uses of the Indefinite Article

Sentence with article	How the article is used
1. A hunter saw a bird in a tree.	before a noun when it is newly introduced.
2. A child cries when he is hungry.	before a noun when it is an example of a class.
3. He drove the car at 60 kilometres an hour.	used in expressions of price, speed. (Means, *per, each*)
4. A Mr. Thomas called when you were away.	*A* means *a person called.*

Some uses of the Definite Article

Sentence with article	Use
1. A man went for a walk with his dog. The man fell into a well and the dog began to bark.	with nouns already mentioned and referred to again.
2. The cycle is the common man's vehicle.	with a singular countable noun which stands for a class.
3. The teacher drew a tree on the blackboard.	before a noun which is the only one of its kind in a given situation. (called the 'unique' *the*)

4. There is a school for the deaf in the city.	before an adjective to turn it into a noun.
5. The Himalayas, the Ganga, the Laccadives, the Indian Ocean	before the names of mountain ranges, rivers, seas, oceans etc.
6. The Nehrus, the Kennedys	to refer to the whole family.
7. Mount Blanc is the highest mountain in Europe.	before adjectives in the superlative degree.

Omission of Articles

Sentence	where omitted
1. Happiness is what everyone longs for.	before an abstract noun. (not omitted when made specific: We must work for the happiness of all sectors of society.)
2. Air and water are indispensable to man.	before mass nouns. (not omitted when made specific: The air in the room is very warm.)
3. Shobha has started going to school. The injured woman was in hospital for a week.	before nouns such as school, college, church, hospital when their primary purpose is implied. (not omitted when they are referred to as places. The postman comes to the school at 11 o'clock. His friends went to the hospital every day to see him.)
4. Man is a social being.	before *man* and *woman* when used in a general sense.
5. He invited me to lunch tea/dinner.	before *lunch, tea*, etc.
6. What sort/type of person is she?	after *sort of, type of, kind of, manner of.*
7. by bus, by plane, by messenger, by post, on foot, by train	before nouns in these phrases.

Exercise 1

Put in *a, an* or *the* wherever necessary and rewrite each sentence:

1. He is poor man. He has wife and children.
2. His eldest child is boy of ten; youngest is girl of two.
3. Everyone likes kind of salesman who is polite to customers.
4. Andamans are group of islands in Bay of Bengal.
5. We travelled by plane at night, flying very high. View from sky was splendid. It was thrilling experience.
6. What happens to all money he earns is a mystery to us.
7. I went to borrow book from library, but librarian was on leave.
8. Number of accidents in city were reported in papers last week. Man was run over by lorry. Woman lost her life in fire. Student fell from moving bus.
9. Atomic power can be great friend or greatest enemy of human race.
10. What fool he was to think that Principal would let him off!

3. PRONOUNS

Personal Pronouns

These stand for *persons*.

		Singular	Plural
1st person:	the person(s) speaking	I	we
2nd person:	the person(s) spoken to	you	you
3rd person:	(an) other person(s) or thing(s)	it he she	they

2 Animals are usually referred to by the pronouns *it* and *they*. Sometimes animals are referred to by the masculine gender when the sex is not specified. When the female sex is specified, it is referred to by the feminine gender.

3 Names of lifeless objects are usually neuter, but cars, loco motives, ships, etc. are often referred to by feminine pronouns.

Pronouns: 'self' form

Here is a list:

myself	ourselves
yourself	yourselves
himself	
herself	themselves
itself	

Reflexive use: I have to blame *myself* for this mistake.
Put *yourself* in my position.
They found *themselves* in great difficulty.

Emphatic use of 'self' form

I offered to drive the car myself.

The -self form emphasizes the noun or pronoun it stands for. It is called an emphatic pronoun. It can emphasize a noun in the object position but not a pronoun.

I saw the Principal himself.
(not *I shall see him himself.*)

Exercise 1

Read these sentences:

He repaired his bicycle.
He did not ask anyone to do it.

We can express the idea in these two sentences in one sentence in the following way:

He repaired his bicycle himself.

Express in one sentence the idea contained in each of the following pairs of sentences, using a suitable self form, as shown above.

1 Let us harvest the rice.
Let us not expect anyone to help us.
2 You do the work.
Don't expect anyone to help you.
3 He painted the windows.
He did not ask anyone to do it.
4 I will clean these rooms.
I won't take anybody's help.
5 They built a fence round the house.
They did not seek anyone's help.

Indefinite Pronouns

Some are born great. *Some* achieve greatness.
Anyone can do this.
Someone called when you were away.
None of the boys answered the question.

The words in italics are indefinite pronouns. Other indefinite pronouns are: *somebody, anybody, something, (the) other, another, nobody, nothing.*

Exercise 2

Fill in the blanks with the pronouns given.

several	many	more	some	both
a few	most	a little	all	

1. A: We must do something about the books missing from the library.
   B: Are there _______?
2. A: Was your father examined by any doctor?
   B: By _______, not one.
3. The child ate all the ice-cream and asked for some _______.
4. _______ of the people is our village live by agriculture.
5. _______ of the critical remarks of the speaker were directed against the government.
6. A: Are all the students present?
   B: Not _______. _______ are absent.
7. 'I don't see Ramu and Balu here. Are _______ of them absent today?'
8. 'Shall I put some sugar in your coffee?'
   'Just _______ please'.

Exercise 3

Fill in the blanks with the interrogative pronouns *who*, *which*, *what*, *whose* and *whom*.

1. '_______ did he say in answer to the question?'
2. '_______ damaged these desks?'
3. '_______ is this portrait?'
4. '_______ disagrees with this proposal?'
5. '_______ of these books would you recommend?'
6. '_______ did you finally elect President?'
7. 'To _______ did you pay the money?'
8. '_______ of Mr. Kumar's sons are you?'
9. '_______ are the consequences of this step?'
10. '_______ is the responsibility to send out the invitations?'

Exercise 4

Fill in the blanks with suitable relative pronouns in their appropriate forms.

1. Tell me the name of the boy _______ won the first prize, in the music competition.
2. I am eager to buy back the house _______ my father sold away ten years ago.

3. 'Uneasy lies the head ______ wears a crown.'
4. That is the man ______ pocket was picked.
5. Which is the boy to ______ you lent your bicycle?
6. The two men ______ had escaped from the prison were caught this morning.
7. The warden has a master key with ______ he can open all the rooms in the hostel.
8. The greedy farmer killed the goose ______ laid the golden eggs.
9. This is a photo of the writer ______ short story I read out to you yesterday.
10. 'Please recommend for this post someone in ______ you have confidence.'

4 ADJECTIVES

Look at these sentences.

A *huge* crowd gathered to hear the Chief Minister. The Chief Minister made a *long* and *impressive* speech.

Huge, long and *impressive* are *adjectives*. They occur between the determiner and the noun.

A Kinds of adjectives

1 *Descriptive Adjectives*

These describe or say something about the condition or quality of the nouns following them. They are of four kinds.

a Adjectives of quality

Shape: round, square, etc.
Size: long, narrow, thick, etc.
Colour: blue, red, etc.
Taste: sweet, sour, etc.

Several other categories can be added to the list.

b Proper adjectives

Indian, French, English, etc.

c Epithet adjectives

passenger train, car factory, etc.

In these a noun functions as an adjective.

d Participial adjectives

a *sleeping* dog, a *wounded* soldier, etc.

In these the present and past participles function as adjectives.

2 *Limiting Adjectives*

Bhaskar and Rahim live in the *same* room.
Nirmala bought *two* saris.

Some and *two* limit the scope of the noun and are called *limiting adjectives*. Here are some more examples.

a Emphasizing Adjectives

I saw the accident with my *own* eyes.
This is the *very* man I am looking for.

b Quantitative adjectives

i *Indefinite adjectives*

One day a riot broke out in the village.
Some words are missing in this paragraph.
Have I made *many* mistakes.?
We hadn't *much* time to spare.

ii *little* and *few*

There is *little* sense in what he says.
Few schools have such a library.

Little and *few* mean *hardly any*.

I have *a little* milk to spare.
There are a *few* Sanskrit books in the library.

A little means *not much* and *a few*, *not many*, but their meaning is positive, not negative.

B Some grammatical items function as adjectives.

Gerund: *dining* table, *walking* stick
Adverb: *upward* trend, *backward* classes
Compound participle: *old-fashioned* clothes, *new-fangled* ideas.

C Adjective: Attributive and Predicative Use

The girl has *lovely* eyes.

Mr Jaleel is a *clever* lawyer.

Lovely and *clever* are adjectives. They state the attributes of the nouns following them. They are said to be used attributively.

The girl's eyes are *lovely*.

Mr Jaleel, the lawyer, is *clever*.

Lovely and *clever* are subject complements and form part of the predicate.

He made his wife *miserable*.

I found him *unreasonable*.

Miserable and *unreasonable* are objective complements and form part of the predicate.

The following are adjectives though they look like adverbs: manly, kingly, friendly, womanly, heavenly.

Kindly can be an adjective or an adverb.

D Positions of adjectives

a) We discussed all matters, *secular* and *religious*.

Adjectives sometimes come after the nouns.

b) Adjectives qualifying indefinite and distributive pronouns come after them.

He always does something useful in his spare time.

Everything necessary will be done.

c) a long, blue ribbon.
   three beautiful, round, red bowls.

When a noun is qualified by a number of adjectives, they appear in this order:

all/both, pronominal adjectives, adjectives of number, adjectives of quality, shape, size, colour, proper adjectives, epithet adjectives.

E Comparison of Adjectives

a. Shoba is a tall girl.
b. Geetha is taller than Shobha.
c. Manju is the tallest of all in the group.

In (a) the adjective *tall* used without any comparison is said to be in the *positive degree*. In (b) the adjective *taller* used to compare two persons is said to be in the *comparative degree*. It is usually followed by *than*. In (c) more than two girls are compared and the adjective *tallest* is said to be in the *superlative degree*.

Note:

i Some adjectives do not have any degrees of comparison. round, perfect, unique.

ii Some comparative adjectives are followed by *to* in place of *than*.

This cloth is superior *to* that.
Mr Pai is senior *to* Mr Kamath.

iii We had a most enjoyable time.
His behaviour was most unfortunate.

There is no idea of comparison here. The superlative only expresses an extreme degree.

2. *Constructions with comparisons*

a. With a positive form we use *as* .... *as*, if the sentence is affirmative.

Murali is as tall as Anand.
When the sentence is negative, we use '*not so/as* .... *as*'.
Shobha is not as/so tall as Geetha.

b. With the comparative form we use *than*.

Geetha is taller than Shobha.

c. When more than two persons/things are compared, we use the superlative.

Raj Kumar is the tallest boy in the class.
Mary is the tallest of all the girls in the class.

d. Study the way the sentences are constructed below.

Raj Kumar is the tallest boy in the class. (superlative)
Raj Kumar is taller than all the other boys in the class. (comparative)
No other boy in the class is as/so tall as Raj Kumar. (positive)

e. Note the difference in meaning between the following pairs of sentences.

Australia is *the biggest* island in the world. (No other island is equal to Australia in size.)
Sri Lanka is *one of the biggest* islands in the world. (There are only a few other islands in the world which are equal in size to Sri Lanka.)

Comparative degree

Australia is *bigger than* all other islands in the world.
Sri Lanka is *bigger than* most other islands in the world.

Positive degree

No other island in the world is as big as Australia.
Only some (a few) islands in the world are as big as Sri Lanka.

j. Prema is not taller than Padma. (comparative degree)
Padma is at least as tall as Prema. (positive degree)

k. Sri Lanka is not the largest island in the world. (superlative degree)
Some islands in the world are at least as large as Sri Lanka. (positive degree)
Some islands in the world are larger than Sri Lanka. (comparative degree)

3 *Use of some comparatives and superlatives*

a. *Elder, older*

Older is used for comparing age and is followed by *than*. *Elder* is not followed by *than* and is used in connection with family relationship.

Anand is the elder of his two sons.
Prema's eldest son is good at music.

b. *Farther, further, farthest, furthest*

Farther and *farthest* are used when distance is referred to.

The railway station is farther from my home than the bus stop.
This is the farthest you can go in a train.
I will take a decision after gathering further information.

Further means *additional*.

c. *Later, latest, latter, last*

Later means *more late* in time.

I cannot wait *later* than Sunday.

Latest means *last up to now*.

The latest news is encouraging.

Latter means: of the two things, the second in the order

Rita and Tara are in the same school.

The former is in class X and the *latter* is in class IX

Last: means final.
The last train leaves at 11.30.

Nearest, next

Nearest expresses distance and *next*, position.

Which is the *nearest* railway station from here?
My house is *next* to the Town High School.

Exercise 1

Fill in the blanks, choosing the right word from those given in brackets.

1. I am _____ than Sridhar. (elder, older)
2. This book is of _____ use to me, so I am returning it. (a little, little)
3. Vinod is much senior _____ me. (than, to)
4. Mr. Menon was the _____ speaker on the resolution. (last, latest)
5. Between Keats and Shelley I read the _____ more often. (later, latter)
6. I have said enough about the subject and I don't wish to say anything _____. (farther, further)
7. The earlier part of the book was dull, but the _____ part was interesting. (later, latter)
8. 'May I ask _____ questions on the subject brought up by you?' (a few, few)
9. His behaviour was _____ odd. (little, a little)
10. 'Let me finish my talk first; I will answer your questions _____.' (later, latter)
11. 'Did you hear the _____ news about the strike?' (latest, last)
12. Mr. Thakore was the _____ man in that village. (oldest, eldest)
13. The _____ you go into that jungle, the riskier it is. (farther, further)
14. We turned on the radio for the _____ news. (latest, last)
15. The post-office is _____ to the co-operative store. (next, nearest)

Exercise 2

Express the meaning of each of the following sentences using the degrees of comparison other than the one you find in it.

1. Bombay is one of the biggest cities in India.

2. The mango is the most popular fruit of India.
3. Abdulla is at least as fast a swimmer as Kesav.
4. This is the most welcome news I have had this year.
5. Ooty is colder than Coonoor.
6. Very few boys in the class are as brilliant as Raghu.
7. China has the largest population of any country in the world.
8. Yesterday was the hottest day we have had this year.
9. Calcutta is bigger than Nagpur.
10. Leela is not a better dancer than Shyamala.
11. These compositions are better than the ones you wrote earlier.
12. I have taken more advice than I have given.
13. He loves all his sons equally well.
14. Gold is one of the heaviest of metals.
15. Is riding the best kind of exercise?

5 VERBS

1. Intransitive Verbs

Fire *burns*.
Ice *melts* at 0°C.

Verbs such as those here do not require objects and are called *intransitive verbs*.

2. Linking Verbs

a Kamala *is* a student in the B.A. class.
The child *appears* happy.
The boy *seems* restless.

The words that follow the verbs are subject complements. The verbs act as links between them and the subjects. Such verbs are *linking verbs*. Since they denote certain states, they are also called *stative* linking verbs. Other similar verbs are: taste, sound, feel, look, remain. They are generally not used in the present progressive tense.

b He is becoming weaker and weaker.
She is growing old.

The verbs are linking verbs of another kind. They denote a process of change and are, therefore, called *dynamic* linking verbs.

3. **Transitive Verbs**

a Nehru liked *children* very much.
My father has written a *novel* in Malayalam.

The verb in each sentence takes an object (given here in italics). Verbs of this kind are called *transitive verbs*. The object answers the question *what*? or *whom*?

b A number of verbs are used with or without objects, that is, transitively or intransitively.

Intransitive	*Transitive*
My father is reading.	My father is reading the newspaper.
The cup broke.	Gita broke the cup.

c

Subject	Verb	Indirect object	Direct object
Father	bought	me	a bicycle.
Mr. Kutty	found	his daughter	a good husband.
Balu	gave	the door	a kick.
The college	awarded	Kamala	a scholarship.

The noun phrases in the last column answer the question 'what?'. They are called *direct objects*. The nouns and the pronoun in the third column answer the question 'to/for whom?' They are called *indirect objects*.

If you want to put the indirect object after the direct object you will have to put *to* or *for* before it.

The college awarded a scholarship to Kamala.
I bought this book for my son.

d. The students elected Prasad *captain*.
We painted the doors *yellow*.

In addition to the objects, the verbs here take complements These complements refer to the objects.

Exercise 1

Rewrite the following sentences putting the indirect object next to the verb, without *to* or *for*.

Examples:
Give the pen to me.
Rewitten: Give me the pen.
Buy a ticket for me.
Rewitten: Buy me a ticket.

1 Can you do a favour to me?
2 Tell everything to me.
3 I have sent two parcels of books to my brother.
4 I have sent my umbrella to Radha.
5 Will you give this note to Kamala?
6 Get a cup of coffee for the patient.
7 Don't promise anything to the boys at this stage.
8 Don't fail to show this report to your father.
9 Could you get a job in your office for my son?

Phrasal Verbs

1 The plane *took off* after repairs.
He *gave up* smoking on my advice.

The verb in each sentence above has an adverb particle after it. The verb and the adverb together form a phrasal verb. Each phrasal verb forms a single meaning unit.

Phrasal verbs can be transitive or intransitive.

Transitive: The soldiers *blew up* the bridge to stop the enemy.
Intransitive: The machine *broke down* and work had to be stopped.

2 The wind blew off his hat.
They called off the match.

The objects (nouns) of the phrasal verbs are put after the adverb particle. If the objects are pronouns, the pronouns are put between the verb and the particle.

The wind blew it off.
They called it off.

3 When the object is a noun, it can be placed either after the particle or between the verb and the particle.
The wind blew off his hat.
The wind blew his hat off.

But this alternative construction is not suitable for some phrasal verbs.

The clerk carried out the instruction.

(*not*, the clerk carried the instruction out.)

Exercise 2

Fill in the blanks in the following sentences with the phrasal verbs given in italics and suitable pronouns in place of the objects.

Examples:

i) Can you make out the writing? No, I can't ____ because I don't know the script.
Answer (make it out)

ii) I rang up Mrs Rao yesterday. I ____ in the evening. *Answer*: (rang her up)

1 The teacher asked the boys to *take down* the new word. The boys ____ in their notebooks.
2 The dentist *pulled out* two of my teeth. He ____ without causing any pain.
3 Mr Lal's cousin *took over* Mr Lal's business after his death. He ____ last month.
4 He *will get back* the money he has deposited after a year. He ____ with interest at 6% per annum.
5 You *should make up* the time you have lost. You ____ by steady and hard work.
6 The principal has *put up* the marks-list on the notice-board. He ____ an hour ago.
7 The magistrate *let off* the young man. He ____ with a warning.
8 The soldiers *blew up* the bridge. They ____ with dynamite.
9 Mr Jayant's publishers are *bringing out* his new novel. They are ____ next month.
10 Parliament *turned down* the minister's proposal. The House ____ by a huge majority.

6 AUXILIARIES AND MODALS

Study the verbs in the sentences below.

1 He *is* going to Calicut tomorrow.
2 I *have* read them all.
3 *Don't* disobey me.
4 *Do* you know the answer to this question?
5 *Is* he attending the wedding?

The verbs in italics *is*, *have* and *do* are used not as full verbs but only as *helping verbs*, to form certain tenses (1, 2), or to make negative sentences (3) or to make questions (4 and 5).

When used in these ways the verbs *be*, *have* and *do* are called *auxiliaries*. They help to form the constructions above.

Modal Auxiliaries

Look at the sentences in this table.

Subject	Auxiliary	Main verb	
Mohan	can	drive.	
You	may	go and play	now.
He	will	take up	the job.
We	shall	be	in Bombay tomorrow.
He	should	see	a doctor at once.
They	would	want	to attend the party.
We	could	get	to the station in time.
The plane	might	arrive	late.
You	must	work	much harder.
You	needn't	worry	about this matter.
He	daren't	face	his father.
You	ought	to obey	the rules.
He	used	to play	tennis.

The words in the second column above are called *modal auxiliaries*. They help to express the mode of the actions denoted by the main verb, such as ability, probability, permission, etc.

Note that it is always the base form of the verb that is used after the modal auxiliary.

If however, the auxiliary *be* or *have* is put after the modal auxiliary the verb can be put in different forms. E.g., He *may be playing*. He *could have said* this.

Uses of Modal Auxiliaries

Modal Auxiliary	Sentence with modal auxiliary	Use
	My brother will arrive tomorrow.	future tense
	Will you please close the door?	polite request
Will	I will come as soon as I am well.	intention/ promise
	We will fight to the finish.	determination
	If you step on a snake, it will bite you.	prediction
	I shall leave for Delhi tomorrow.	The future when the subject is *I* or *we*
Shall	He shall report for duty tomorrow.	a command or threat when used with the second and third persons.
	Shall I make a cup of coffee for you?	an offer/suggestion when used with *I/we* in questions
	He can speak four languages including French.	ability
Can	You can go home now.	permission
	Accidents can happen to anyone.	possibility

May	You may collect your notebooks. May I borrow your dictionary?	permission
	It may rain this evening	possibility
	May he live long!	a wish
Would	Every morning Gandhiji would go for a walk.	a habitual activity in the past.
	Would you care for a glass of lime juice?	a suggestion/enquiry
	Would you please close the door?	polite request
	I would rather starve than beg.	a wish/preference when used with *rather*
	I would like to ask you something.	a wish when used with *like*
	He said he would look into the matter.	used as the past tense of *shall* or *will* in indirect speech
Should	I said that we should report for duty on Monday.	The past tense of *shall* in indirect speech
	People should not tell lies.	obligation
	You should take regular exercise.	advisability
	They should be home by now.	logical inference/ probability
	Should I see him, I will speak to him.	expressing a probable condition

	He said that the results might appear in the next day's papers.	the past tense of *may* in indirect speech
Might	It might rain.	remote possibility (remoter than *may*)
	Might I make a suggestion?	permission in question (implies more politeness than *may*)
	He said he could finish the book in a day or two.	the past tense of *can* in indirect speech
Could	I could read without glasses until three months ago.	ability in the past
	Could you wait for a minute?	polite request
	If we had the money, we could buy that house.	possibility under a certain condition
Must	The letter must leave by today's mail.	obligation, compulsion, necessity (For the past, we use *had to*.)
	If this is litmus paper, it must turn blue.	logical necessity or expectation

There are two negatives for *must*.

a You needn't bring your certificates. (absence of obligation)
You don't have to stay.

b You mustn't walk on the grass. (not permitted to)

Need

a A: Must I answer all the questions?
B: You needn't. You need answer only six questions.

Needn't expresses the idea that there is no compulsion. In this sense it is the opposite of *must*.

b *Need* I wait any longer?

Need is used this way in interrogative sentences.

Need as a modal does not have a past tense form. The past tense is expressed by *need have/need not have*.

Need I have come to the party?

You need not have come.

Ought

You ought to obey orders.

You ought not to speak ill of others.

Ought expresses duty. The *verb* that follows *ought* takes the to + verb form.

Dare

How dare you say such a thing?

I daren't leave without permission.

Dare is used to express fearlessness of any consequence.

(The expression *I dare say* means *it seems to me probable or likely*.)

Used to

a He used to go for a walk every morning.
(Now he doesn't.)

Used to + verb expresses a habit in the past. It doesn't have a present tense form.

b There used to be a park in this place long ago.

Used to be expresses the existence of something in the past.

(He is used to a hard life. *Used to* here means '*accustomed to*'.)

Exercise

Fill in the blanks with modals appropriate to the meaning indicated in brackets.

1. You must be leaving now. I _____ meet you at the railway station. (future)
2. You _____ come to the party, won't you? (future)
3. I _____ walk twenty-five kilometres in five hours. (present ability)
4. You _____ leave those papers on my desk and go.(permission)
5. I am afraid the weather _____ not improve for another two or three days. (probability)
6. You _____ be able to see him if you hurried up. (slight possibility)
7. You _____ not hide from them what they should know. (moral obligation)

8. You _____ go (permission), if you _____. (compulsion)
9. If he _____ (ability) come as far as my neighbour's house why _____ (ability) he come to mine?
10. He _____ apologise or face the consequences. (command)
11. You _____ ask for any more leave for the rest of the year. (prohibition)
12. If you _____ put in a word to the manager, I _____ be very grateful. (polite request)
13. I _____ wait (willingness) if I _____. (obligation)
14. You _____ (duty) take the initiative and do things.
15. You _____ wait (advisability) till you are asked to do something.
16. It _____ rain soon, or the crops will die. (necessity)
17. You _____ come to see me in my office. It is enough if you give me a ring. (absence of compulsion)
18. _____ we go to Malampuzha for the picnic? (suggestion)
19. He _____ tell his father the whole truth. (absence of courage)
20. Gokhale and Tilak _____ sit for hours together talking and Gandhiji _____ sit and listen eagerly. (habitual action in the past)
21. We _____ not go abroad to learn English; we can learn it well right here. (absence of compulsion)
22. I _____ rather stay at home than go for a walk in this weather. (preference)

7 ADVERBS AND ADVERBIAL PHRASES

1 *Formation*

a) Adverbs are usually formed by adding /ly/ to the corresponding adjectives. In the case of adjectives ending in /y/, the /y/ is changed to /i/.

In the case of adjectives ending in /c/ /ally/ is added. *Publicly* is an exception. In the case of adjectives ending in /able/ or /ible/, /e/ is dropped and /y/ is added.

b) *deep, early, far, fast, high, hard, late, low, little, much, near*. These can be used both as adjectives and as adverbs.

2. *The Comparison of Adverbs*

a. Satisfactorily | more satisfactorily | most satisfactorily

With adverbs of two or more syllables, the comparative is formed by putting *more* before the adverb, and the superlative by putting *most*. *Less* and *least* are used for negative comparisons.

b. To single syllable adverbs and the adverb early we add /er/ and /est/.

fast	faster	fastest
hard	harder	hardest
early	earlier	earliest

c. These adverbs have irregular forms for the comparative and the superlative.

well	better	best
little	less	least
much	more	most

3. *Constructions with comparisons*

a. The woman spoke as angrily as the man.
For the positive degree we use *as .... as* in an affirmative sentence and *not so/as .... as* in a negative sentence.

b. The party ended earlier *than* I had expected. For the comparative degree we use *than*.

c. He ran fastest (of the six runners).

For the superlative degree we use *of* + noun/pronoun. *Of + noun* can also be implied as in c. above.

He acted *most* foolishly.

Most here means *very*. No comparison is made.

5 *Adverbs and Adverbial Phrases*

A	B
The soldiers fought *very courageously*.	The soldiers fought *with great courage*.
The defeated army surrendered *unconditionally*.	The defeated army surrendered *without laying down any conditions*.
I searched for the missing umbrella *everywhere*.	I searched for the missing umbrella *in all places*.
I thank you *whole-heartedly*.	I thank you *with all my heart*.

The words in italics under A are adverbs. Under B they have been replaced by adverb phrases. This is possible with a large number of adverbs.

Exercise 1

Rewrite the following sentences substituting adverbs for the adverb phrases given in italics.

1 The beggar waited at my door *with patience*.
2 He does any work given to him *with sincerity and earnestness*.
3 The Principal thanked the staff and students *with all his heart* for their cooperation.
4 He listened to us *with great indifference*.
5 The boys listened to the talk *with great attention*.
6 He acted *in a thoughtless manner*.
7 Sridhar is *without doubt* the brightest boy in the class.
8 He spoke *with great eloquence*.

Exercise 2

Rewrite the following sentences putting the adverbs and adverbial phrases given in brackets in suitable places. Make any other changes that may be necessary.

Mrs Das: Arun got up this morning. (at six o' clock)
Mr Das: That is what he does. (always)
Mrs Das: I'd like him to get up. (at five o' clock every day)
Mr Das: That is what he will do. (never)
Mrs Das: He must read four hours a day. (at least)
Mr Das: You can't get him to read four minutes. (hardly)

Mrs Das: He is intelligent. But it is difficult to make him work. (fairly, rather)
I hope he will get a second class. (at least)

Mr Das: There is little chance of his passing. (scarcely)

Mrs Das: It is easy to say that. (too) There is time for him to work hard and make up. (still)

Mr Das: What will you say? (else)
There are only about three months for his final examination. (hardly)

Mrs Das: You encourage no one. (hardly ever)

Mr Das: And you discourage no one. (seldom)

Mrs Das: Why should I say a harsh word? He is old to see things for himself. (enough)

Mr Das: If he did! (only)

8 PREPOSITIONS

1 There is a temple *on* that hill.

The word *on* is a preposition and *that hill* is its object. *On that hill* is a prepositional phrase.

2 Most prepositions are single word ones such as *in, on, at, for, about, against, above, below, notwithstanding*, etc. They are called simple prepositions.

3 The following words are used like prepositions though they look like verbs or adjectives.

excepting	barring	considering
concerning	following	including
granted	pending	like
worth	save	unlike
plus	minus	

4 There are a number of phrases which are called *complex prepositions*.

Examples:

along with, apart from, as for, such as, except for, owing to, due to, but for, because of, by means of, on account of, in comparison with.

Positions of prepositions.

A preposition is usually put before the noun it governs. It is also sometimes put in other positions.

The teacher has a chair to sit *on*.
This is the book I told you *about*.

Exercise 1

Fill in the blanks with appropriate prepositions.

1 This year's College Day was celebrated ________ February.
2 It was celebrated ________ the last day of the month.
3 The District Collector presided ________ the College Day function.
4 The collector arrived exactly ________ 5 p.m.
5 He was received ________ the Principal and the Union President and conducted ________ the dais.
6 He was one of the distinguished old boys ________ the college.
7 He took his seat ________ the Principal and the Union President.
8 The programme began ________ a prayer song sung ________ a group of girls.
9 The Principal then read the report ________ the year.
10 The report dealt ________ the curricular and extra-curricular activities ________ the year.
11 ________ his report, the Principal thanked the staff and the students ________ the co-operation extended ________ him.
12 The Collector ________ a brief speech, congratulated the staff and the students ________ their excellent record for the year.
13 He appealed ________ the students to concentrate ________ their studies while ________ college.
14 The Union President proposed a vote ________ thanks.
15 He said the college could be legitimately proud ________ such distinguished old boys as the chief guest.
16 The meeting was followed ________ a programme ________ variety entertainment.

Exercise 2

Fill in the blanks with suitable prepositions.

1 The secret ________ success lies ________ planning ahead and ________ hard work.
2 By just putting one's faith ________ fate one cannot hope to gain much.

3 He didn't give any reply ________ my question.
4 His stories are full ________ humour.
5 He seems to be always ________ a hurry.
6 The Principal will be ________ leave ________ two months ________ the 15th of this month.
7 Some managements find themselves ________ the mercy ________ the trade union leaders.
8 There was an acute shortage ________ food that year ________ account ________ the failure ________ the monsoon.
9 The room was filled ________ the sweet smell of roses.
10 Man does not live ________ bread alone.
11 He has a large circle ________ friends.
12 The municipality is planting trees ________ the main roads.
13 We had to travel ________ several hours ________ jungles before we arrived ________ the village.
14 People spend too much money ________ decorations, lighting, etc. ________ weddings.
15 The cave men produced fire ________ rubbing two stones ________ each other.
16 The twins look so exactly alike that you can't distinguish one ________ the other.
17 ________ my way back I will call ________ the hospital and see our friend.
18 If you want to be admitted ________ the MBBS course, you should get a first class in your P.U. Examination.
19 A very experienced doctor is attending ________ my father.
20 Mr Roy lives ________ a big house ________ Tambaram.
21 Don't worry ________ finding your way ________ my home. I will write down the instructions ________ full ________ you.
22 I find the family always quarrelling ________ themselves.
23 Since the prisoner was hard ________ hearing, questioning him ________ detail was not easy.
24 Ashok disapproved ________ my plan ________ our picnic, but Mohan sided ________ me. I did not quarrel ________ Ashok, since everyone is entitled ________ his opinion.

Exercise 3

Fill in the blanks with the phrasal prepositions given.

except for	at variance with	in spite of
in aid of	in addition to	in view of
in accordance with	for the sake of	

1 Your essay has been well written ———— a few factual errors.
2 I am forced to cancel my trip abroad ———— my present health.
3 ———— being treated by the best doctors, he did not show any signs of improvement.
4 His evidence in the court was ———— what he had said to the police.
5 A mother will undergo any amount of suffering ———— her child.
6 She was buried by the side of her husband's grave ———— her wishes.
7 The old boys collected Rs. 50,000 ———— the college building fund.
8 He was given the portfolio of Agriculture ———— the portfolio of Education.

Exercise 4

Fill in the blanks with suitable prepositions.

1 My friend reminded me ———— our appointment this evening.
2 The police had to resort ———— force in order to disperse the violent crowd.
3 I have severed all connections ———— that party.
4 The judge convicted the accused ———— murder.
5 The manager approved ———— my suggestion.
6 You should read the instructions in the question paper carefully and comply ———— them.
7 He wants to dispose ———— his house and build a new one.
8 Mr Misra endowed the college ———— a lakh of rupees in memory of his father.
9 We should not put up ———— this kind of treatment.
10 Mr Roy, our neighbour, has invited us ———— dinner tomorrow.
11 I must apologise ———— you ———— this mistake.
12 Indian poets often compare a beautiful face ———— the full moon.
13 The President congratulated the Indian hockey team ———— its splendid victory.
14 Very young children depend ———— their parents ———— all their needs.
15 The clerks grumbled ———— the low pay they were getting.

16 Have you informed the police ———— the theft?
17 The young man insisted ———— marrying the girl of his choice.
18 The conductor objected ———— the dog being taken into the bus.
19 I prefer coffee ———— tea.
20 He is recovering from an attack ———— typhoid.
21 The police suspected the man ———— being a smuggler.
22 The notice warned motorists ———— the danger ahead.

Exercise 5

Fill in the blanks with suitable prepositions.

1 The police are responsible ———— the maintenance of law and order.
2 I am quite satisfied ———— your work.
3 The bus ran short ———— petrol and stopped.
4 Tobacco in any form is injurious ———— health.
5 The management was indifferent ———— the representations of the workers.
6 Our hostel is adjacent ———— the college.
7 Climbing a high mountain peak is beset ———— many difficulties and dangers.
8 'Be content ———— what you have.'
9 His life was dedicated ———— the service of the poor.
10 The tourist was not familiar ———— the customs of the country.
11 'I am grateful ———— you ———— all your kindness.'
12 His written statement was not consistent ———— what he had said earlier.
13 He was not acquainted ———— the language I spoke.
14 The parents of the child became anxious ———— his safety. when he did not return home with the other children.
15 The judgement of the High Court was favourable ———— the government.
16 King Midas was greedy ———— gold.
17 He was found guilty ———— neglect of duty and was dismissed.
18 Good health is indispensable ———— happiness.
19 Is not learning preferable ———— wealth?
20 That building was not suitable ———— a school.

Exercise 6

Fill in the blanks with suitable prepositions.

1 The Minister expressed his concern ________ the people affected by the floods.
2 My knowledge ________ this subject is limited.
3 We have already taken a decision ________ this matter.
4 Our connection ________ that business was severed many years ago.
5 He has no capacity ________ sustained work.
6 'Please pay attention ________ what I am going to say.'
7 'What is the basis ________ your charge?'
8 King Dasaratha was a descendant ________ King Raghu.
9 'There is an exception ________ every rule.'
10 Fifty members voted ________ favour ________ the resolution
11 We have no hope ________ finding our lost dog.
12 He has a knack ________ saying the right things at the wrong time.
13 Raghu is no match ________ Sunil in table-tennis.
14 He was in great need ________ money for his daughter's wedding.
15 'Have you any objection ________ my coming in dhoti and shirt?'
16 Mohan's progress ________ his studies was not very satisfactory.
17 The clerk made a request ________ a month's leave.
18 The accident was the result ________ rash driving.
19 Mohan's teacher expressed his surprise ________ Mohan's failure.
20 Several persons were witness ________ the fight between the two rowdies.

9 CONJUNCTIONS AND CONNECTORS

A Kinds of conjunctions

1 *Co-ordinating conjunctions*.

Look at the italicized conjunctions in the sentences in column A and their functions mentioned in column B

A	B
a Men *and* women	joins two nouns
b He spoke loudly *and* clearly.	joins two adverbs
c She wore black *and* white beads.	joins two adjectives
d The frog can live in water *and* on land.	joins two adverbial phrases.
e He learnt to drive *and* to repair cars.	joins two infinitives
f Boys who are absent *and* don't send in a leave-letter will be fined.	joins two clauses

Conjunctions like *and* are co-ordinating conjunctions. Other co-ordinating conjunctions are: *or, for, but, still, yet, so, otherwise, nor, neither, as well as*.

2 *Correlative Conjunctions*

He must be *either* a fool *or* a knave.

I can *neither* read *nor* speak Urdu.

I can't say *whether* he will come *or* not.

The pairs of conjunctions are related to each other and are called *correlative conjunctions*. Other similar conjunctions are: *so*.......*as*; *such*........*that*: *both*.......*and*: *though*.......*yet*; *not only*........*but also*; *no sooner*.......*than*.

3 *Subordinating conjunctions*

I don't think *that* he is right.

Tell me *where* you have put my watch.

The words in italics are conjunctions which help to connect subordinate clauses to main clauses. They are called subordinating conjunctions.

Here is a list of subordinating conjunctions:

why, how, when, though, although, since, after, until/till, as, because, before, than, if, unless, while, whether, lest, so that, as if, as long as, as soon as.

Exercise 1

Fill in the blanks with the conjunctions given. You may have to use some of them more than once.

and, yet, but, nor, or, as well as, so, otherwise, neither, for.

1 'I am very tired. Give me a cup of coffee _____ tea.'
2 There are sixty boys _____ twenty girls in this class.
3 Mohan is tall, _____ his brother is short.
4 We need to have rains very soon, _____ the crops may wither up.
5 His uncle gave him a good education _____ money to start a business.
6 We should be kind to all living creatures, _____ they are all creations of God.
7 He has never told a lie, _____ will he ever do so.
8 We bought this car only last month, _____ it has started giving trouble already.
9 He didn't send in a leave-letter, _____ he was marked absent.
10 The day dawned, _____ birds began to chirp in the trees.
11 He is very rich, _____ he is not happy.
12 'I'll come and see you, _____ I'll give you a ring.'
13 The house had no running water, _____ it had electricity.
14 'I'm not hungry now, _____ I'll eat my dinner later.'

Exercise 2

Fill in the blank in each sentence below, with the conjunction (single word or phrase) that pairs with the one italicized.

1 '*Neither* a lender _____ a borrower be.'
2 He says he can't decide *whether* to marry _____ not.
3 The coffee was *so* hot _____ it scalded my tongue.
4 'Nothing is *so* irritating _____ a good example,' said Mark Twain.
5 There was *such* a heavy downpour in the morning _____ the entire playground was covered with knee-deep water.
6 *Both* Mr Das _____ his wife have been abroad.
7 The robbers *not only* robbed the travellers _____ beat them up.
8 *No sooner* did the teacher enter the class _____ the boys stood up.
9 The food in the hostel was _____ very good *nor* very bad.

10 'I'm going to marry this girl, _____ you like it *or* not,' said the young man to his elder brother.
11 'These mangoes are not _____ nice *as* the ones we bought yesterday.'
12 'I have never eaten _____ nice mangoes *as* these.
13 'I have known _____ Ramu *and* his brother since their boyhood.'
14 He _____ got a first class in his M.A. examination *but also* stood first in the University.
15 _____ had the speaker begun his speech, *than* a man stood up to ask a question.

10 THE TENSES: FORM AND USE

Uses of Present Simple [base form + s]

Examples	The tense expresses
a Mohan *gets up* every day at five in the morning.	habitual action.
b Water *boils* at 100°C.	a permanent truth.
c Sugar *costs* Rs. 6 a kilo.	a fact that exists at the time of speaking.
d Asok *passes* the ball to Ravi and Ravi *throws* it right on the stumps.	events actually going on, (as in running commentaries)
e I *leave* for Delhi tomorrow. I *return* to Hyderabad next Monday.	planned actions in the future.
f (Portia appealed to Shylock to have mercy on Antonio, but Shylock rejected her plea.) Now Shylock *comes forward* with a pair of scales and a knife. He *moves* towards Antonio.	a past event in a vivid or dramatic manner.

The Present Continuous Tense (am, is, are + verb + ing)

Examples	The tense expresses
a The children *are playing* in the garden.	an action that is in progress.
b My father *is writing* a book.	an action in progress but not necessarily at the moment of speaking.
c I *am meeting* the Chief Minister tomorrow morning.	an action in the near future.
d The boys *are always complaining* about the food.	with *always, constantly, regularly,* etc., a repeated action (often with a suggestion of disapproval).

A number of verbs are not normally used in the present continuous tense:

i verbs of perception: see, hear, smell
ii verbs which express feelings/states of mind: want, desire, wish, refuse, forgive, care, hate, like, dislike, admire
iii verbs involving the process of thinking: think, feel, know, mean, suppose
iv verbs denoting possession: have, own, owe, belong, possess
v verbs such as: contain, consist, keep, cost, seem

When some of the verbs listed above are used in the -ing form, the meanings change.

We hear several rumours about the missing M.P.	The judge is hearing the case tomorrow. (conducting)
I think this time he will pass.	He is thinking seriously of resigning. (considering)

Exercise 1

Fill in the blanks with the simple present or the present continuous forms of the verbs given in the brackets. Choose the form for each verb according to the meaning of the sentence.

1 The boys generally _____ to their uncle's house for the holidays, but this year they _____ there. (go, not go)

2 My nephews _____ here tomorrow. They usually _____ their vacation here. (arrive, spend)

3 I _____ some light literature, such as novels and short stories during my vacations. (read)

4 He generally _____ a gray suit, but today he _____ a white one. (wear, wear)

5 He rarely _____ an umbrella, but he _____ one now. (carry, carry)

6 Ravi _____ his homework still. His brother who always _____ quicker has finished his and _____ in the garden. (do, work, play)

7 I _____ you _____ a copy of *Airport*. How do you like the book? (notice, have)

8 Ask the man what he _____ (want)

9 "You _____ to enjoy this film, I don't really." (seem)

10 "I usually _____ to college. But today I _____ in my brother's car." (walk, go)

11 A: Who _____ that funny noise? (make)
B: It is our uncle. He _____ his nose. (blow)

12 Those two boys who _____ each other so strongly are my nephews. They _____ medicine. (resemble, study)

13 Don't disturb him, he _____ . (work)

14 Children _____ to play on the sand. (love)

15 "I _____ what his name is." (forget)

Uses of the Simple Past (verb +ed/t)

Examples	The tense expresses
a Every day he read a few chapters of the Gita. Every day he went for a walk.	habitual or regular action.
b He lived in Delhi for ten years.	an action in the past (which occurred during a period of time) which is now ended.
c My father left for Delhi yesterday.	an event that occurred at a particular time in the past, usually used with an adverb/adverb phrase.

The Present Perfect Tense

Look at these sentences.

The children *have eaten* all the sweets.
(There are no more left.)
The old tenant *has vacated* the house.
(I must look for another.)

The verbs are said to be in the present perfect tense. The form is *has/have* + the past participle; ***have eaten*, *has vacated***.

The tense expresses actions and events completed in the past. But what is said has current relevance, some link with the present. The sentences in brackets show the nature of the link.

Examples	The tense expresses
a I *have seen* the Taj Mahal.	an experience in the past.
b He *has lived* in this house for twenty years. They *have been* here since six o'clock.	an action which began in the past and continues still. (*for* is used to indicate length of time and *since* to indicate a point of time.)
c He *has found* a job.	an action completed in the past (with current relevance).

Look at these sentences and note the difference between the Simple Past and Present Perfect.

Mr Kapoor lived in Delhi for fifteen years. (He does not live there now.)
Mr Kapoor has lived in Delhi for fifteen years. (He still lives in Delhi.)

Exercise 2

Fill in the blanks in each item below with the correct forms (the past tense or the present perfect form) of the verb given in brackets.

1 I _____ this book; I _____ it last month. (read)
2 I _____ its author; I _____ him at a conference in Madras. (see)

3 My father _____ several books. He _____ his eighth novel last month. (write, finish)

4 A: Where is Ganesh?
B: I _____ (not see) him after he left home in the morning. He _____ (tell) his mother this morning that he would be in for lunch.

5 Shopkeeper: Do you know that lady who _____ (just leave) the shop?
Customer: Yes, that is Miss Thorat. Why?
Shopkeeper: She _____ (be) here several times but she never _____ (buy) anything.

6 An hour ago someone _____ (ring) up the airport and _____ (say) that there _____ (be) a time bomb in the Jumbo jet. The police and the crew of the plane are searching for it but so far they _____ (not find) anything. This is the third time they _____ (have) a scare like this.

I _____ my lunch. I _____ it half an hour ago. (have, have)

8 All the guests _____. They _____ half an hour ago. (leave, leave)

9 I _____ to bring my English textbook.
I _____ to bring it yesterday too. (forget, forget)

10 I _____ all my life in this village and at 84 I don't want to leave it and go to a city. (live)

11 I _____ my spectacles. Can you help me to find them? (mislay)

12 He and I are great friends. We _____ each other for thirty years. (know)

Exercise 3

Complete the following sentences with each of the two endings given, using *since* or *for*, whichever is right, in the blanks.

Example: We have had a severe drought in our state _____
(a) a year (b) January last

a) We have had a severe drought in our state for a year.

b) We have had a severe drought in our state since January last.

1 They have been in this town _____.
a) quite a long time.
b) 1900.

2 I haven't smoked a cigarette ——.
  a) the day my teacher advised me against it.
  b) the last 15 years.
3 My brother hasn't sent us any money ——.
  a) the beginning of the year.
  b) ten months now.
4 We haven't written to each other ——.
  a) nearly a year.
  b) last January.
5 He has worn the same suit ——.
  a) two weeks
  b) the beginning of this month.

Past Progressive Tense.

Look at these sentences:

Once a hunter *was walking* through a forest. Suddenly he saw a tiger in front of him.
I *was ironing* my shirt when the electricity failed.

The verb is in the *past progressive* or *past continuous* tense. The form of the verb: *was/were + verb + ing*. The tense expresses an action in progress in the past.

Uses

Examples	The tense expresses
1 At 8.30 a.m. I was having my breakfast.	an action in progress at a point of time in the past.
2 The boys were listening to the cricket commentary the whole of yesterday.	an action in progress over a period of time in the past.
3 The train was crossing the bridge when the bridge gave way.	a continuing action at some point of time in the past when another action took place.
4 While some boys were reading in the library, the others were playing in the playground.	two or more actions going on at the same time (conjunction *while* is used).

Some adverbs used with the past progressive tense are: *always, continually, constantly, forever,*

She was always scolding her children.
He was continually coming late.

Note the position of the adverb.

Exercise 4

Fill in the blanks with the simple past tense or past continuous tense forms of the verbs given, so as to make meaningful sentences.

1 Ravi _____ some letters, when I _____ to see him, (write, go)
2 He _____ across the road when a bicycle _____ him. (walk, hit)
3 She _____ her finger when she _____ potatoes. (cut, slice)
4 The lights _____ when we _____ at dinner. (go off, be)
5 As he _____ the bus, it _____ with a jerk. (get off, start)
6 Mother _____ into the kitchen and _____ that the milk _____ over. (go, find, boil)
7 While the priest _____ the sermon, some people _____ out of the window. (preach, look)
8 He _____ his pen while he _____ yesterday evening. (lose, play)
9 The doctor _____ (have) his morning coffee when the telephone rang.
10 The nurse _____ (tell) the doctor that the patient _____ (need) his attention immediately.
11 He _____ (drive) very fast when a policeman _____ (stop) him.
12 The man injured in the accident _____ (bleed) badly when the doctor _____ (arrive) on the scene.

Past Perfect Tense

Look at these sentences:

On reaching the school, I found *I had forgotten* to bring my English text-book.

When we reached the theatre, the play *had begun* already.

The verbs in these sentences are in the *past perfect* tense. The form is: had + past participle. There are two actions in each sentence above, both taking place in the past. The earlier action (or event) is expressed in the past perfect tense and the later action in the simple past.

Uses

Examples	The tense expresses
1 By the time the police arrived on the scene, the dacoits *had fled*.	an action in the past completed before another action, also in the past.
2 At nine o' clock the plane *had left*. When he wrote to me about the result, I *had alredy known* it from the newspapers.	an event that happened earlier, when looked at from a point of time in the past.
3 I did not know the man because I *had not seen* him before.	an action/event in the past which denotes causes for later actions in the past.
4 I wish I *had accepted* the job. (But I did not accept it.)	an unfulfilled wish referring to the past.
5 If he *had worked* hard he would have passed. (He did not work hard and he failed.)	an unfulfilled condition in the past.
6. When he *had received* the prize, he sat down.	an earlier action, to dispel the impression that the two actions happened at the same time. (Compare *when he received the prize* he sat down.)

Exercise 5

Match each of the statements under A with a sentence made from table B. In each sentence you have to make from the table, the first column and the last column are fixed for you. You have to find the suitable words from the second and third columns. The first one is done for you, as an example.

A

Mother was very tired. (Matching sentence: She had worked all day.)
I had to clean the vessels myself.
We were late for the show.
Raju said he wasn't hungry.
The students collected their notebooks.
The manager wanted to make some changes in his letter.

B

She		corrected	all day.
The maid		begun	them.
The show	had	cleaned	already.
He	hadn't	posted	a snack.
The teacher		had	their compositions.
Luckily the peon		worked	it.

Exercise 6

Fill in the blanks with the simple past or the past perfect forms of the verbs given in brackets, to make the sentences meaningful.

1 By the time the doctor _____ the patient _____. (arrive, die)
2 The teacher _____ they could go home when they _____ the work assigned to them. (say, complete)
3 We _____ the poem after the teacher _____ it to us. (understand, explain)
4 Several hours before the match _____ the spectators _____ the stadium. (begin, fill)
5 I wish you _____ your application by the due date. (submit)
6 Jain _____ to get a first class. He _____ only a second class and was naturally disappointed. (hope, get)
7 They _____ hungry because they _____ nothing to eat since the previous evening. (be, have)

8 I _____ my friend for many years, and he _____ a lot; so when I _____ him last week I _____ him at first. (not see, change, meet, not recognize)

Exercise 7

Combine each of the following pairs of sentences using the past perfect tense to express the earlier action or event.

Examples:

a The film began at 9.30 p.m.
We reached the cinema hall at 10 p.m.
When we reached the cinema hall, the film had already begun.

b He joined his father's business.
He was then nearing twenty years of age.
By twenty he had joined his father's business.

c I did not see him for many years.
I did not recognise him at once.
I did not recognise him at once because I had not seen him for many years.

1 The train left at 8.
We reached the station at 8.15.

2 I went to bed.
The telephone rang a minute later.

3 The fire burnt down all the huts.
The fire engine arrived later.

4 Mother made the coffee.
We woke up a little later.

5 The bell rang.
Soon after, the teacher entered the classroom.

6 The sun rose.
The traveller woke up sometime later.

7 He took his M.A. degree.
He was then nearing 18 years of age.

8 The typist typed eight letters.
A little later it was 11 o'clock.

The Present Perfect Continuous Tense

Look at these sentences:

Mr George *has been teaching* in this college for ten years.
I *have been having* a pain in my back ever since the accident.

The verb is in the *present perfect continuous tense*. The form is: *has/have + been + verb + ing*.

Uses

Examples	The tense expresses
1 I *have been living* in this house since 1940.	an action/event that began sometime ago, and is still going on.
2 I feel cold because I *have been swimming* for an hour.	an action which was going on till a recent point of time and whose result is still present.

We can use the present perfect tense in place of the present perfect continuous tense in several cases.

I *have lived* in this house/ *have been living* in this house for five years.

Exercise 8

Fill in the blanks with the suitable forms (present perfect or present perfect continuous) of the verbs given in brackets.

1 I _____ to him again and again but _____ from him yet. (write, not hear)
2 I _____ you for a long time. What _____ all these days? (not see, do) (Supply the subject in the question.)
3 That lime tree _____ near our house ever since I was a boy. I'm glad no one _____ it down. (stand, cut)
4 These boys _____ English for three years now. (learn)
5 They _____ the house and _____. (lock up, go away)
6 The boys _____ ten kilometres and are now resting. (walk)
7 'You _____ a lot lately. You ought to do something about it.' (cough)
8 The workers _____ for a rise in their wages for a year now, but they _____ to go on strike on this account. (agitate, not dare)

Past Perfect Continuous Tense

Look at these sentences:

The telephone bell *had been ringing* for five minutes, but there was no one to attend to it.

The verb is in the *past perfect continuous tense*. The form is: ***had** been + verb + ing*.

The past perfect continuous tense expresses an action/event that had begun and was going on upto a point of time in the past.

Exercise 9

Make sentences from the table below to match the clues. The clues are given in the same order as the sentences to be made from the table. The first one is done for you as an example.

Clues

1 The bus came at last. (Matching sentence: We had been waiting for it for an hour.)
2 The workers decided to go on strike yesterday.
3 Mohana showed me a sweater.
4 Mr Jain was transferred from Bombay to Calcutta.
5 Fatima got the first rank in the examination.

1 We		knitting it for two months.
2 They		working in Bombay for five years.
3 She	had been	waiting for it for an hour.
4 He		working hard for this success.
5 She		demanding a rise in their wages.

The Future Tense

English verbs don't have a special form for expressing future time. Instead there are several ways of expressing it.

a I *shall return* your book on Monday.
You *will know* your result in a day or two.

The future is expressed with *shall* or *will* + the verb. *Shall* is used with the first person and *will*, with the second and third persons. In current usage *will* is also used with the first person to express the future.

b Our cricket team *leaves* for Bombay this evening. They *play* two matches there.

The present simple is used to express a series of planned actions in the future.

c The Director of Collegiate Education *is visiting* the college tomorrow.

The present continuous tense is used to express an anticipated event in the near future.

d I *am going to buy* a new bicycle.
He *is going to fail* if he wastes his time like this.

The 'going to' phrase is used to express the speaker's intention to perform a future action (as in the first sentence) or an action that is expected to take place (as in the second sentence).

e The train is *about to leave*.

About to + verb expresses events whose happening is imminent.

f I *am to be* at a meeting at 5 o'clock.
Mr John *is to preside* over this year's College Day.

The form *be* + *to* + *verb* is used to express a duty or necessity or a planned course of action in the future.

Exercise 10

Fill in the blanks in the sentences given below, using the verbs in brackets, in one of the ways that express the future.

1 I find an extra plate on the table. Who _____ to dinner? (come)
2 We have telephoned to the police. They _____ here any moment. (be)
3 I _____ at home next week. I _____ for Delhi tonight. (not be, leave)
4 There are dark clouds in the sky. I think it _____. (rain)
5 'The roof has caught fire. I'm afraid it _____. Stand back.' (fall)
6 My programme: I _____ office in the forenoon.
I _____ for Madras by the 2-30 plane.
I _____ my business in Madras in an hour and _____ the 6-30 plane back to Hyderabad. (attend, leave, finish, take)
7 Mr Ahmed _____ present at the meeting next week. He _____ abroad. (not be, go)

8 'Isn't it too hot inside?'
'I _____ the windows if you like.' (open)
9 Did you see the notice on the notice-board? The annual examinations _____ on the 15th. They _____ on 31st March and college _____ the same day for summer vacation. College _____ on 15th June. (begin, end, close, reopen)
10 Mr Dhar _____ here only till 2 p.m. He _____ at two for a meeting. He _____ over it. (be, leave, preside)
11 He hasn't been working at all. He _____ in the examination. (fail)
12 I have bought some nice curtain material. I _____ some curtains for the doors and windows. (make)
13 The Chief Engineer is examining the bridge. They _____ it. (repair)
14 He has let his house on rent. He _____ to Madras. (go away).

The Future Continuous Tense

I have to hurry up. Padma *will be waiting* for me.

The verb is in the *future continuous tense*. The form is: *shall* +*will* +*be* + *verb* + *ing*.

Uses

a A fresh stock of saris *will be arriving* next week.

The tense is used to express an event expected to take place in the future in the natural course.

b When I reach Calicut, it *will be raining* there.

The tense expresses an action/event that is expected to be in progress at a point of time in the future.

The Future Perfect Tense

I *shall have typed* all the letters by six o' clock.

The verb is in the *future perfect* tense. The form: *shall* + *will* + *have* + *past participle*.

Uses

a I *shall have finished* writing this book by the end of next week.

The verb expresses an action expected to be completed by a certain time in the future.

b 'You *will have heard* about our plans for the Diamond Jubilee of our College', the lecturer said to the students.

The tense is used here to express not the future but the speaker's belief that the students have heard about the plans.

Exercise 11

Make sentences from table B to match the sentences under A. The first one is done for you as an example.

A

1 The half-yearly examination will be held in December. (Sentence: The class will have completed ten lessons by then.)
2 Come at 8 o' clock for your dinner.
3 The fire engine will take at least half an hour to get here.
4 You can reach the railway station before ten.
5 How can you expect the tailor to give you your suit next Monday?
6 How can I hope to buy a house after retirement.?
7 We no doubt have some debts.

B

1 The class 2 I 3 The fire	will/shall have	destroyed all the huts by then. made it by then. saved enough money for a house.
4 The train 5 He 6 I 7 But we	will/shall not have	completed ten lessons by then. cooked the dinner by then. paid them off by the end of next year. left by that time.

11 NEGATIVE AND INTERROGATIVE SENTENCES

Negative Sentences

1 Look at the sentences in A and B.

A	B
He was interested in politics.	He was not (wasn't) interested in politics.
The schools have been closed.	The schools have not (haven't) been closed.
They're tourists.	They're not tourists.

Note the following:

i) *Not* is added to affirmative sentences to make them negative sentences. ii) The *not* comes between the auxiliary and the main verb (is *not* interested) iii) Contracted forms (haven't, aren't) are common in spoken English.

2 He comes here every day.
Mr David went to Bombay yesterday.

In these sentences the verb is present simple or past simple and hasn't got any auxiliary. The negative sentences are formed in these cases by introducing the auxiliary *do* and adding *not* to it.

So we have the following negative sentences:

He does not (doesn't) come here every day.
Mr David did not (didn't) go to Bombay yesterday.

3 Look at the sentences in A and B.

A	B
Do it again.	Don't do it again.
Come here tomorrow.	Don't come here tomorrow.

When imperative sentences are put in the negative form, the auxiliary *do* is used with the negating word *not*, the contracted form (*n't*) being used more often.

He hadn't any money. (*or* He didn't have any money.)
He hasn't any money. (*or* He doesn't have any money.)

In these sentences the verb *have* is used as a full verb. It is made negative by adding the contracted form /*n't*/ to it.

Exercise 1

Complete the following sentences with the verbs given in brackets, putting them in the appropriate tense form and in the negative.

Examples:

a Ravi has borrowed a book from the library, but he _____ reading it. (start)
Ravi has borrowed a book from the library, but he hasn't started reading it.

b He sat for the examination but he _____ it. (pass)
He sat for the examination, but he didn't pass it.

1 He has done four years' research, but he _____ his degree yet. (get)
2 If you _____ a taxi, you will miss your train. (take)
3 In spite of his earnest request they _____ the question of his promotion. (reopen)
4 The lady looked at dozens of saris, but _____ any. (buy)
5 'I _____ anywhere. I just came here to see a friend off.' (go)
6 'If the weather there _____ with you, you may come back.' (agree)
7 'Your face is familiar, but I _____ your name.' (remember)
8 Although he _____ in the house, he pays the rent regularly. (live)
9 I used to play cricket regularly, but I _____ for the last five years. (play)
10 She has been dieting for the last six months, but _____ much weight. (lose)

5 Look at these sentences:

I *seldom* go to the pictures.
He *rarely* speaks at public meetings.
He has *little* knowledge of the subject.
He is a shy type and has *few* friends.
He was *barely* sixteen when he took his B.A. degree.
There is *scarcely* any rice in the house.
There is *hardly* any logic in his arguments.

The words in italics are negative in meaning. They are followed by words such as *any, anything, anywhere*, rather than words such as *some, something, somewhere*.

Interrogative Sentences

Yes-or-No Questions

a Look at these sentences:

A	B
This is the road to the University.	Is this the road to the University?
All the rooms are vacant.	Are all the rooms vacant?
They have a car.	Have they a car?
There is a canteen in the college.	Is there a canteen in the college?

The sentences in A are *statements*. Those in B are *questions*. The verb in each sentence in B here comes first and the subject is put after it. In other words, there is an *inversion* of subject and verb.

b Look at these sentences:

A Statements	B Yes/No Questions
He works in the Corporation office.	Does he work in the Corporation office?
They go to the park every evening.	Do they go to the park every evening?

For questions in B the auxiliary *do* or a form of it is provided in questions and it is put before the subject.

c i Did you see my brother anywhere here?
ii Did you see my brother somewhere here?
i Is anyone absent?
ii Is someone absent?

Notice the difference between (i) sentences and (ii) sentences. In the latter the speaker tends to believe that the answer is 'yes' but not so in the former.

d i Can't you tell the truth?
(I thought you would, but it seems you won't.)
ii Aren't you ashamed of your conduct? (You ought to be, but it appears you are not.)

Note the meaning of each sentence above which begins with an

Exercise 2

The following is the report of a conversation between a lawyer and a witness during the trial of a case. Only the witness's answers are given and you have to frame the questions the lawyer may have asked to get the answers given. The witness gives only short answers, the rest being unsaid or understood. The understood or unsaid portions are in the brackets and they will help you to make the lawyers's questions.

Examples:

Lawyer: .... ?
Witness: No, I am not. (a weaver)
Answer: Are you a weaver?

Lawyer: .... ?
Witness: No, I'm not. (related to Mr. Shah)
Lawyer: .... ?
Witness: No, he isn't. (a friend of mine)
Lawyer: .... ?
Witness: Yes, I do. (know him)
Lawyer: .... ?
Witness: No, he hasn't. (lent me money)
Lawyer: .... ?
Witness: Yes, he does. (charges high interest)
Lawyer: .... ?
Witness: Yes, he did. (lend money to the prisoner)
Lawyer: .... ?
Witness: Yes, I was. (at the prisoner's shop on 30th September)
Lawyer: .... ?
Witness: Yes, he (Mr Shah) was. (there at that time)
Lawyer: .... ?
Witness: Yes, he (prisoner) did. (stab Mr Shah)
Lawyer: .... ?
Witness: Yes, I did. (see the stabbing)
Lawyer: .... ?
Witness: Yes, he did. (use a knife)
Lawyer: .... ?
Witness: Yes, it is. (the knife I saw)
Lawyer: .... ?
Witness: Yes, I am. (quite sure)

Tag Questions

Look at these sentences:

Mr Keskar is at home, isn't he?
It rained yesterday, didn't it?
They aren't coming to visit us, are they?
The train hasn't left, has it?

Each of these sentences consists of a statement and a short question separated by a comma. The short question is called a *tag question*. In such questions the speaker is only asking for confirmation of his statement.

Also note that an *affirmative statement* takes *a negative tag*, and a *negative statement* takes an *affirmative* tag.

He is coming to the show, isn't he?
He is not coming to the show, is he?

Exercise 3

Add appropriate tag questions to the following sentences. Remember to separate the tag by a comma.

1 We are travelling by train.
2 Mr Jacob has invited us to dinner.
3 Kashmir summers are wonderful.
4 A large number of tourists are expected this year.
5 You haven't booked our tickets.
6 You hope to get tickets for all of us.
7 You don't want me to come with you.
8 Mr Prasad is giving us a talk on Electronics this evening.
9 Our team hasn't won a single match.
10 None of the girls liked the entertainment.

Question-Word Questions or Information Questions

a Look at these questions:

Why is this a difficult problem?
Where are you working now?

These questions are called question-word questions or information questions. They begin with question-words such as *when, why, where, how, who, what,* etc. and ask for some information.

Note how question-word questions are formed:

Statement	*Yes-or-no form*	*Question-word form*
You are working now.	Are you working now?	Where are you working now?
This is a difficult problem.	Is this a difficult problem?	Why is this a difficult problem?

We first form a yes-or-no question and then put the appropriate question-word before it.

---

b He ate *a mango*.
Mr Rao returned from Madras *last Monday*.
The prisoner escaped *by scaling the wall*.

To get the information, italicized in each statement above, we make these questions.

What did he eat?
When did Mr Rao return from Madras?
How did the prisoner escape?

c Study these information questions, made with phrases formed by the question-word *how* joined to an adjective or adverb.

Statements	*Questions*
The prison wall was twenty feet high.	How high was the prison wall?
There are two colleges in the district.	How many colleges are there in the district?
The postman comes here three times a day.	How often does the postman come here?
This book costs ten rupees.	How much does this book cost?

d Question-word questions with *who, which* and *what*, when these words stand for the objects in the sentences, are made a shown below.

i The maid broke the plates.
What did the maid break?

ii They invited the judge.
Who/whom did they invite?

iii She chose the red sari.
Which sari did she choose?

iv That is Sekhar's house.
Whose house is that?

e The maid broke the plates. — Who broke the plates?
The black book is mine. — Which book is yours?
This happened in Bombay. — What happened in Bombay?

In these sentences the question-word replaces the subject and so becomes the subject in the question. In such cases there is no subject-verb inversion.

If the question-word replaces the object, inversion takes place.

He was talking to his neighbour.	Who was he talking to? To whom was he talking?
He left out the last question.	Which question did he leave out?
He wants ice cream.	What does he want?

f Look at these statements/answers and study the form of the questions.

Statements/Answers	*Questions*
I want a knife for mending the pencil.	What do you want a knife for?
I dipped it in milk.	What did you dip it in? (*or* In what .....)
I am buying this for my son.	Who are you buying this for? (*or* For whom ....)

Exercise 4

The conversation between the lawyer and the witness is continued below. This time the questions of the lawyer are question-word questions. The question-words with which his questions begin are given.

Make the questions.

Lawyer: Where .... ?
Witness: I saw it on the counter in the prisoner's shop.
Lawyer: When .... ?
Witness: I saw it on 29th September.

Lawyer: Why .... ?
Witness: I went (to the shop) to buy some meat.
Lawyer: How .... ?
Witness: (I know this was the knife) because it has the same kind of handle.
Lawyer: What kind .... ?
Witness: It was a kitchen knife.

---

12 THE PASSIVE VOICE

A Look at these sentences.

1 A committee of lecturers prepared the College Annual Report.

2 It was read by the Principal on College Day.

Sentence 1 above says what the committee did: they prepared the report. *A committee of lecturers* is the subject of the sentence and the verb expresses the action performed by *them*. The verb is transitive and its object is the noun *report*. The verb is in the *active voice*.

In Sentence 2, the verb, *was read*, does not express an action done by the subject, but only the action that the report 'received' or 'suffered'. The form, *was read*, is used to express the idea. Verbs in this form are in the *passive voice*.

1 *When to use the Passive Voice*

Look at these two sentences:

The Principal read the report.
The report was read by the Principal.

There is practically no difference in the meaning or idea expressed by the two sentences.

But this is not always so. Often sentences in the active voice and those in the passive voice express a difference in emphasis.

Look at these two sentences:

The Panchayat dug a well to provide water to the village.
A well was dug to provide water to the village.

Here we would prefer to use the second rather than the first sentence, if what we want to refer to is not the action of the Panchayat but the result of the action, namely, a well being provided in order to supply water to the village.

Here are two more examples of contexts in which the passive voice is preferred.

A bridge was built across the river. (Who built it is not important.)
A mistake was made in totalling the marks. (Who made the mistake is not our concern here, but only the occurrence of the mistake.)

The passive voice is used in preference to the active voice, in describing a scientific or technical process. For example: Common salt is got from the sea. Sea water is collected in salt pans. It is allowed to evaporate in the sun. As a result, salt crystals are formed at the bottom. They are removed and dried in the sun.

B Now look at these sentences:

The electric bulb was invented by Edison.
Hamlet was written by Shakespeare.

In these sentences the *by + noun (agent)* phrase is necessary to complete the meaning. If the *by + agent* phrase is not needed for completing the meaning, it is not used. We would say: 'The house was sold for Rs. 35,000' and not 'The house was sold for Rs. 35,000 by its owner'.

C The form of the passive

Active	*Passive*
a This shop sells radios.	a Radios are sold in this shop.
b The servant washes our clothes.	b Our clothes are washed by the servant.

Note the changes we have made to transform sentences from the active voice to the passive.

a We put the object of the active verb in the subject position. For example 'radios,' the object, is made the subject in sentence a.

b The form of the verb is changed in the passive: *sells* becomes *are sold*.

c The number of the verb is changed according to the number of the noun in the subject. For example: *Sells* becomes *are sold*.

d i Note the passive forms of verbs used in different tenses:
Present simple: Rows of lamps *are lighted* on that day.
Past simple: The books *were sold out*.
Present continuous: Houses *are being built* for Harijans.
Past continuous: The papers *were being corrected*.
Present perfect: The house *has been whitewashed*.
Past perfect: The questions *had been given out*.
Future simple: Rows of lamps *will be lighted* on that day.
Future perfect: The votes *will have been counted* by then.

ii. Note the passive forms of the modals below:
can: The prize can be won by Mohan.
may: The car *may be stopped* at the end of this road.
could: The car *could be driven* by electricity.
must: A reply *must be sent* without delay.
should: He *should be seen* by a doctor at once.
ought: Elders *ought to be shown* due respect.
may have: The clothes *may have been washed* by now.
must have: The cakes *must have been* eaten by the boys.
need: This *needn't be attended to* now.

Exercise 1

Rewrite the following sentences in the passive voice. Use the *by + agent* phrase only where it is found necessary.

1 Alexander cut the Gordian knot.
2 A Committee makes the selection of students.
3 The lecturer marks the attendance every period.
4 The auditors are checking the accounts.
5 The police are investigating the murder.
6 The Reception Committee has made all the arrangements.
7 Mother has cooked the dinner.
8 The cat drank all the milk.
9 The enemy bombed the city last night.
10 The chairman was ringing the bell.
11 The students were decorating the college hall.

12 The General Body had passed two of the resolutions.
13 The Municipality had sanctioned the construction of the theatre.
14 The Principal will interview the students in the afternoon.
15 A high court judge will conduct the enquiry.
16 He will have completed it by the end of next month.
17 They will have announced the results by the beginning of June.
18 We have posted most of the invitations.
20 They have added two hundred books to the library.

D *Passive of Commands*

Look at these sentences:

Send these letters by registered post.
Inform the police of the accident.

Commands such as these are put in the passive as follows:

Let these letters be sent by registered post.
Let the police be informed.

The form of the verb is *let + be + past participle*, and the subject is put between *let* and *be + past participle*.

E *Passive of questions*

1 Look at these sentences:

Do they speak Malayalam?
Can we send this big parcel by air?
Must we cut this tree?

Yes-or-no questions such as these are put in the passive voice as follows:

Is Malayalam spoken by them?
Can this big parcel be sent by air?
Must this tree be cut?

Notice the form of the passive voice question. It is: *modal auxiliary + be + past participle*.

2 Look at these question-word questions:

Where did you buy this pen?
Why did they pull down the building?
When do they deliver the mail?

These information questions are put in the passive as follows:

Where was this pen bought?
Why was the building pulled down?
When is the mail delivered?

Exercise 2

Put the following sentences into the passive voice. Use the *by + agent* phrase only where necessary.

1 Type these letters before 4 o' clock.
2 Deposit this money in the bank.
3 Send invitations to all the parents.
4 Do you take colour photos?
5 Did they hire a bus?
6 Is the doctor examining the patient?
7 Where do they play the match?
8 Why did they raise this question?
9 Where can you get some petrol?
10 When do they clear the mail?
11 Who broke the news?
12 What did they discuss at the meeting?
13 We can't take up this work now.
14 Some persons don't eat onions.
15 The tourists didn't visit this place.

F Look at this sentence:
The police gave him a reward of Rs. 1,000.

It has two objects, the indirect object *him*, and the direct object *a reward of Rs. 1,000*. The sentence can be rewritten in the passive voice by making either of the objects the subject of the sentence and retaining the other object.

a He was given a reward of Rs. 1,000 by the police.
b A reward of Rs. 1,000 was given him by the police.
c A reward of Rs. 1,000 was given to him by the police.

Sentence (a) above reads more natural and is often preferred.

Exercise 3

Put each of the sentences below into the passive voice, in the three ways shown in the example.

Example:

Active voice:

Mr Kumar teaches us English.

Passive voice:

We are taught English by Mr. Kumar.
English is taught us by Mr. Kumar.
English is taught to us by Mr. Kumar.

1 The manager refused the clerk leave.
2 Someone showed me the photograph.
3 Why did they give him so much money?
4 My uncle gave me a good education.
5 You should teach the man a lesson.

Exercise 4

Put the sentences below into the passive voice as shown in the example.

Example:

Active voice:

The accident left the man a cripple.

Passive voice:

The man was left a cripple by the accident.

1 Woollen clothes keep us warm.
2 The children called Nehru '*Chacha*'.
3 We have painted the house green.
4 They named the child Dinesh.
5 The judge found the prisoner not guilty.

Exercise 5

Put the sentences below into the passive voice as shown in the example.

Example:

Active voice:

The teacher permitted the boys to go and play.

Passive voice:

The boys were permitted by the teacher to go and play.

1 The principal asked the boy to wait.
2 The doctor advised the young man to give up smoking.
3 You can help me to solve the problem.
4 The constable saw a man throwing a stone.
5 He taught me how to face an interview.

Exercise 6

Put the sentences below into the passive voice, as shown in the example.

Example:

Active voice:

The discovery surprised the researcher.

Passive voice:

The researcher was surprised at the discovery.

1 We have notified the workers.
2 The agreement satisfied the workers.
3 Social work interests Mrs Das very much.
4 The news surprised everyone.
5 The admission work engaged the Principal the whole day.

13 NON-FINITES

Look at these sentences.

1 He wants *to buy* a new house.
2 *Buying* a new house needs money.
3 I found him *looking for* a new house.
4 *Shaken* by the experience he was ill for a few days.

To buy in sentence (1), *buying* in the sentence (2), *looking for* in sentence (3) and *shaken* in sentence (4) are forms of verb called *non-finites*. They have none of the tenses, have no number and take no modals.

To buy is an infinitive;
Buying is a gerund;
Looking for is a present participle;
Shaken is a past participle.

The Infinitive

1 Look at the forms of the infinitive in the following sentences:
a Jaya wanted to learn photography.
b She is reported to be learning it.
c She is reported to have learnt painting already.

In these sentences you see three forms of the infinitive.

2 The infinitives shown above have the word *to* before them.
But in these sentences *to* is omitted:

The mother made the child *drink* the medicine.
Then she let the child *go* out to play.

This omission takes place after certain verbs. They include: make, let, see, hear, watch, have, bid.

3 Look at the sentences in A and B.

A	B
We saw him leave.	He was seen to leave.
I heard the postman knock at the door.	The postman was heard to knock at the door.

Note that in A the verbs are in the active voice and take the bare infinitive. When the verbs are put in the passive voice in B the infinitives take *to* before them.

4 Look at these sentences:

He is too young to go to school.
He spoke too fast to be followed.

In these sentences the infinitive is used with *too + adjective/ adverb*. The sentences can be transformed into complex sentences using *so ...... that*.

He is so young that he cannot go to school.
He spoke so fast that he could not be followed.

Exercise 1

Rewrite the following sentences using *to*, wherever necessary, before the infinitives given in brackets.

1 Mrs Bose asked her son _____ home before 8 o' clock. (come)
2 If you have planned _____ the airport before five, you had better _____ at once. (reach, start)
3 He wouldn't let anyone _____ his bicycle. (use)
4 We wanted _____ the house where Mahatma Gandhi was born. (see)
5 Did you really see him _____ you brother? (beat)
6 We were not permitted _____ the hospital. (enter)
7 He would rather _____ than _____ a lie. (die, tell)
8 He made us _____ for an hour. (wait)
9 I would have him _____ again for this purpose. (come)
10 You needn't _____ all the questions. (answer)

Exercise 2

Combine each of the following pairs of sentences using *too* followed by an infinitive.

Example:

The grapes were very sour.
We couldn't eat them.
The grapes were too sour to eat.
or
The grapes were too sour for us to eat.

1 He was very weak.
He could not walk.

2 You are very young.
You cannot be admitted to college.
3 He was very proud.
He wouldn't talk to us.
4 This lesson is very long.
It cannot be finished today.
5 He is very honest.
He could not have told a lie.
6 This news is too good.
It cannot be true.

The Gerund

The gerund and the present participle have the same form *verb* + *ing*: swimming, walking, cutting, etc.

1 *Examples of uses of the gerund*

a Swimming is a good exercise.
Smoking in the auditorium is prohibited.
b He likes reading detective novels.
Would you mind waiting for a few minutes?
c He inaugurated the school by lighting a lamp.
He was fined for being drunk while driving.
d Talking to him is *wasting* time.
Seeing is *believing*.

Look at the *-ing* form in these sentences
He has a collection of walking sticks.
He bought a new dining table.

Note the meaning of the gerund in this use. For example, *walking stick* means not a stick that walks, but a stick for walking.

2 Some verbs usually take the infinitive after them, some take the gerund and some others take both the infinitive and the gerund. Below are two examples of verbs that take the infinitive.

She consented to marry the man.
We decided to start the work.

A few other such verbs are: *expect, manage, pretend, choose, offer*.

Here are some examples of verbs which usually take gerunds:

He *acknowledged making* a mistake.

He *admitted (to) telling* a lie.
She *avoided seeing* the principal.
I *considered approaching* the minister.
He *denied using* force.

Some other such verbs are: *dislike, enjoy, favour, finish, help, mind, postpone, stop, suggest.*

The verbs listed below can take either the gerund or the infinitive, though with some the infinitive is more frequent and with the others the gerund.

can't bear, begin, cease, continue, dislike, dread, fear, forget, hate, intend, like, love, mean, neglect, prefer, propose, recollect, regret, remember, start, try.

Exercise 3

Fill in each blank with the correct form (either gerund or infinitive) of the verb given in brackets.

1 I hope ——— this time. (pass)
2 He managed ——— the station in time. (reach)
3 Don't forget ——— the lights before ——— to bed. (switch off, go)
4 Would you mind ——— a little? (wait)
5 Please stop ——— ; you are disturbing the others in the library. (talk)
6 I don't mind ——— . (come with you)
7 I tried my best ——— the great man, but missed ——— him. (interview, see)
8 If we don't have all the facts, I suggest ——— our decision. (postpone)
9 I never meant ——— his order. (disobey)
10 I don't think he is ill, he is only pretending ——— ill. (be)

Participles

The present participle or active participle

Look at the words in italics in these sentences.

We found a child *crying* for its mother. *Calling* the child to us, we gave it some sweets.

The words in italics are present participles. The form is *verb + ing*
The gerund has also the same form.

1 *Examples of the uses of the present participle*
a A *drowning* man catches at a straw.

An astrologer professes to predict *coming* events.

His behaviour is *irritating*.
His speech was *illuminating*.

b *Seeing* the policemen, the crowd dispersed.
He entered, *closing* the door behind him.

In these sentences two actions by the same subject are referred to, one following the other. The earlier action is expressed by the present participle.

c He went into the bathroom *singing*.
He walked away *whistling*.

In these sentences the two actions referred to occur simultaneously and one of them is expressed by the present participle, which functions as an adverbial.

d Look at this sentence.
We found him *watering the plants* in his garden.

The participle functions as object complement in this sentence.

e The weather *being fine*, we decided to go for a walk.
In this sentence the participle and the verb of the main clause have different subjects. In cases like this the participle must follow the noun/pronoun which is its subject.

2 *Having seen* my brother off, I came home.
In this sentence *having + the past participle of the verb* is called a 'perfect participle'. The perfect participle is used to show that the action expressed by it is completed before the second action referred to in the sentence starts.

3 *Having been duped* once, he did not fall into the trap again.

In this sentence the perfect participle is used in the passive voice. The form is: *having + past participle of 'be' + past participle of verb.*

The Past Participle

The verbs in italics in the sentences below are in the past participle form and have a passive meaning. They have the same uses as the present participles.

a His *spoken English* is much better than his *written English*.

The Chief Minister arrived, *accompanied* by the Minister for Education.

b They became *tired*.
We felt *bored*.

The past participles are subject complements in the above sentences.

c We found all the chairs *damaged*.
I got a new shirt *made*.

The past participles are used as object complements in these sentences.

Exercise 4

Combine each of the following pairs of sentences using either a present participle or a perfect participle. Make the italicized sentences in each pair into a participle phrase.

Example:

a *They left the car on the road.*
They walked into the jungle.
Leaving the car on the road, they walked into the jungle.

b *She fed the cow.*
Then she milked her.
Having fed the cow, she milked her.

1 *I felt pity for the beggar.*
I gave him some money.
2 *Bhima raised his club.*
He struck a heavy blow.
3 *I had seen the play once.*
I had no desire to see it a second time.
4 *She fed the children.*
Then she sat down to her lunch.
5 The lion jumped into the well.
He mistook his own image for another lion.
6 *He had already told a lie.*
He had to tell several more lies in support of it.
7 *They had taken a decision.*
They wanted to stick to it.
8 *We have decided to fight.*
Let us fight.

14 DIRECT AND INDIRECT (REPORTED) SPEECH

1 Look at the sentences given below.

'How have you done your English paper?' John asked Raju.
'I have done it quite well,' said Raju.

In these sentences the words spoken are repeated exactly as they were spoken, and quotation marks enclose the words. This form of reporting is called *direct speech*.

Here is another way of reporting the same conversation:

John asked Raju *how he had done his English paper*. Raju said *that he had done it quite well*.

Here, what is said is reported with some changes in grammatical construction. The changes are made in the verb, pronoun, etc. and are made from the point of view of the person reporting and the time and place of reporting. This form of reporting is called *indirect speech* or *reported speech*.

2 The verb *said* above is called the 'reporting' verb. The reporting verb we use in indirect speech depends on the kind of sentence reported. For example:

Direct speech: 'Please give me five paise,' the beggar *said* to the passer-by.
Indirect speech: The beggar *begged* the passer-by to give him five paise.

Similarly we use *affirm, declare, protest*, etc. in statements; *order, tell*, etc. in commands; *ask, enquire*, etc. in questions and *exclaim, cry*, etc. in exclamations.

3 Here are some examples of how the four types of sentences can be put into indirect speech:

a *Statements*

Direct speech: Ravi said, 'The English lecturer will be on leave for a week.'
Indirect speech: Ravi said (*that*) *the English lecturer would be on leave for a week*.

Direct speech: 'The annual examinations will begin on 15th March,' the principal said.

Indirect speech: The principal announced *that the annual examinations would begin on 15th March*.

The statement is changed into a *that*-clause, also called a noun clause.

b *Commands and requests*

i *Positive*

Direct speech: The General said to the squadron leader, 'Bomb the enemy's ammunition factories.'

Indirect speech: The General *ordered* the squadron leader *to bomb* the enemy's ammunition factories.

Direct speech: 'Please grant me leave for a day,' the clerk said to the manager.

Indirect speech: The clerk *requested* the manager *to grant* him leave for a day.

Commands and requests are reduced to phrases by changing their verbs to infinitives with *to*. An appropriate reporting verb is used.

ii *Negative*

Direct speech: 'Please don't touch the exhibits,' the guide said to the students.

Indirect speech: The guide *requested (asked)* the students *not to touch* the exhibits.

c *Questions*

i *'yes-no' questions*

Direct speech: The man asked, 'Can I withdraw the money whenever I need it?'

Indirect speech: The man *enquired if he could withdraw the money whenever he needed it*.

Direct speech: 'Didn't I tell you to take the patient's temperature every hour?' the doctor asked the nurse.

Indirect speech: The doctor *asked the nurse whether he hadn't told her to take the patient's temperature every hour*.

'Yes-no' questions are changed into noun clauses beginning with *if* or *whether*.

ii *Question-word questions*

Direct speech: 'What did you eat for breakfast today?' the doctor asked the patient.

Indirect speech: The doctor *asked* the patient *what he ate (had eaten) for breakfast that day*.

Question-word questions are reported by turning the question into noun clauses beginning with the question-word. The subject and the verb are put back in the normal statement order.

d *Exclamations*

Direct speech: 'What a splendid building!' the tourist said when he saw the Taj.

Indirect speech: The tourist *exclaimed*, when he saw the Taj, *that it was a very splendid building*.

Exclamations are often changed into statements in reported speech. Note the use of *very* to bring out the desired emphasis or the intensity of the exclamation.

4 *Sequence of tense in reported speech*

In reported speech the reports are most often concerned with what was said in the past. By the time we make our report, the events we talk about are over. The reporting verbs are therefore usually in the past tense: Mohan *said* that .... ; Mohan *asked* .... Note the changes in the tenses that take place in indirect speech when the reporting verb is in the past tense.

a Direct Speech: 'I don't eat meat,' my guest said.
Indirect Speech: My guest said *that he did not eat meat*.

b Direct Speech: 'Are you taking back all your money?' the clerk asked the man.
Indirect Speech: The clerk asked the man whether he *was taking back* all his money.

c Direct Speech: 'You have spoken a lie,' Mr Das said to his servant.
Indirect Speech: Mr Das said to (told) his servant that he *had spoken* a lie.

d Direct Speech: 'The visitor has been waiting for an hour to see you, sir,' the peon told the Manager.
Indirect Speech: The peon told the Manager that the visitor *had been waiting* for an hour to see him.

e Direct Speech: 'The Manager will call you after an hour,' the peon said to the visitor.
Indirect Speech: The peon said to the visitor that the Manager *would call* him after an hour.

f Direct Speech: 'I shall return from Delhi on Monday,' my neighbour said.
Indirect Speech: My neighbour said that he *would return* from Delhi on Monday.

g **Modals**

Direct speech: Ravi said, 'I posted the letter.'
Indirect speech: Ravi said that he *had posted* the letter.
Direct speech: The teacher said to the boys, 'You may go home.'
Indirect speech: The teacher said to the boys that they *might* go home.
Direct speech: 'Can you ride a bicycle?' I asked Gita.
Indirect speech: I asked Gita whether she *could* ride a bicycle.
(In Indirect speech the modals are changed into their corresponding past forms.)

Note the following exceptions to the rule:

a Direct speech: The teacher said, 'Our country became independent in 1947!'
Indirect speech: The teacher said that our country became independent in 1947.

b Direct speech: He said, 'If Ravi approached me, I would certainly help him.'
He said that if Ravi approached him he would certainly help him.

c Direct speech: He said, 'When the Principal walked in, the teacher was not in the class.'
Indirect speech: He said that when the Principal walked in, the teacher was not in the class.

In (a) the speaker refers to a historical event.
In (b) an imagined condition is expressed.
In (c) two actions occurring at about the same time are expressed.

In such cases the *past tense* remains unchanged in the indirect form. Similarly, there is no change in the following:

Direct Speech: He said, 'God is everywhere.'
Indirect Speech: He said that God is everywhere.

Direct Speech: He said, 'I go for a walk every morning.'
Indirect Speech: He said he goes for a walk every morning.

Direct Speech: Mr Patil said this morning, 'I am going to buy a car soon.'
Indirect Speech: Mr Patil said this morning that he is going to buy a car soon.

The present tense in direct speech is not changed into past tense if the sentence spoken expresses a universal truth, a habitual action, or a fact that is true at the time of reporting. The future tense, similarly, is not changed into the past form, if what is said refers to the future at the time of reporting. See the last example above.

5 Now look at the following sentences.

Direct Speech: Ravi says, 'I met Mr. Rao at the railway station.'
Indirect Speech: Ravi says that he met Mr Rao at the railway station.

Direct Speech: Mohan will say, 'I want two persons to assist me.'
Indirect Speech: Mohan will say that he wants two persons to assist him.

When the reporting verb is in the present tense or future tense the verbs undergo no change in indirect speech.

6 *Reported speech: Change of person*

Direct Speech: The doctor asked the patient, 'Did *you* eat anything this morning?'
Indirect Speech: The doctor asked the patient whether *he* had eaten anything that morning.

Direct Speech: '*I* ate bread and a few biscuits,' replied the patient.
Indirect Speech: The patient replied that *he* had eaten bread and a few biscuits.

Notice that the pronouns above are changed from the point of view of the person reporting. *I* and *you* become *he*. When the person reporting is neither the speaker nor the man spoken to, *I, we, my, our, you, your*, etc. are changed to *he, him, his, her, they, them, their*, etc.

Now look at these examples:

Direct Speech: I asked the policeman, 'Can you tell me the way to the station?'

Indirect Speech: I asked the policeman whether he could tell me the way to the station.

Here, the person is reporting his own words. So *me* is not changed to any other pronoun. In all these cases the pronouns are changed in reported speech from the reporter's 'point of view,' that is, according to who the reporting person is. The other changes indicated below also follow the same principle, that is, they depend on who the reporting person is, what the time of reporting is and where the reporting takes place.

7 *Other changes*

Demonstratives and adverbials

In most cases, words denoting nearness in time and place are changed into words denoting distance. The changes made are:

Direct Speech	*Indirect Speech*	*Direct Speech*	*Indirect Speech*
this/these	that/those	tomorrow	the next day
here	there	yesterday	the day before
now	then	ago	before, earlier
today/ tonight	that day/ that night	next week	the following week
last week	the previous week		

Examples:

Direct Speech	*Indirect Speech*
Mohan: I must go to the library today and return this book.	Mohan said he had to go to the library that day and return that book.
Ashok: Can't you return it tomorrow?	Ashok asked Mohan whether he couldn't return it the next day.

Mohan: I can't, because yesterday was the last day for keeping the book.	Mohan replied that he couldn't, because the day before was the last day for keeping the book.

Exercise 1

Rewrite the following statements in indirect speech.

1 'We are moving into a new house,' my neighbour said.
2 'If it rains we will have to cancel the match,' the captain said.
3 'We shall go to the zoo,' Ashok said to his friend.
4 Hassan said to me, 'I will see you tomorrow.' 'I am not free tomorrow,' I said to Hassan.
5 'Those who have written the essay can go home,' the teacher said.
6 All my friends tell me, 'You will be a great man one day.'
7 'I have been waiting for an hour,' complained Ashok.
8 My friend said, 'You may have my bicycle if you want to use it. I shan't be needing it for two days.'
9 'Your husband will soon be well. Let him be in bed for a week,' Dr. Sapru told Mrs Rao.
10 'I am going to Delhi on the 10th. The interview is on the 14th,' Kasim said.

Exercise 2

Rewrite the following in indirect speech.

Example:
Arun said to Ravi, 'Please lend me your dictionary.'
Arun asked (requested) Ravi to lend him his dictionary.

1 Mr Rao said to his wife, 'I may be late for dinner. Don't wait for me.'
2 'Raju,' said Raju's mother, 'don't tell lies. Tell me the truth.'
3 The captain said to the soldiers, 'Don't fall back. Keep firing and advancing.'
4 The Gita says, 'Do your duty. Don't worry about the results of your actions.'
5 'Don't argue with your father,' Mrs Das said to her son.
6 'Wear a false beard and no one will know who you are,' my friend advised me.
7 'Taste a little of this. Tell me if I have put too much salt in it,' she said to her daughter.
8 'Don't talk loudly. You will disturb the baby,' my aunt said.

9 'Be careful. The steps are slippery,' my friend said to me.
10 'Get me some paper and a pen,' my father said to me.

Exercise 3

Rewrite the following in indirect speech.

Example:

Doctor to patient: Do you have a headache now?

The doctor asked the patient if he had a headache then.

1 Shop-keeper to lady: 'Do you want the red sari or the green one?'
2 I to policeman: 'Can you tell me the way to the hospital?'
3 Parent to teacher: 'Will my daughter pass or fail?'
4 My neighbour to me: 'Are you going to Delhi next week?'
5 Ravi to Raju: 'Shall we plan a picnic for next Sunday?'
6 Father to son: 'Hasn't the postman come yet?'
7 Mother to me: 'Have you watered the plants?'
8 Secretary to visitor: 'Who(m) do you want to see?'
9 Mr Munshi to me: 'Whose portrait are you painting?'
10 Uncle to me: 'When does the postman come every day?'
11 Mrs Das to Mr Das: 'How many people are coming to dinner?'
12 Inspector to prisoner: 'Where did you get these counterfeit notes from?'

Exercise 4

Rewrite the following in indirect speech.

1 'What a pleasant evening! Shall we go for a walk?' said Ravi to his friends.
2 'How stuffy it's here! Let's go out and sit in the garden,' Prema said to her friends.
3 'How nice of you to have come!' my friend said to me.
4 'How persuasively your lawyer argued the case!' my friend said to me.
5 'What a pity you did not come to the party!' my friend said to the girl.
6 'What a lazy girl you are! How shabbily you have done your work!' the teacher said to Judy.
7 'May God bless you!' said the old man to the boy.
8 'What shall I do now?' cried the traveller, whose pocket had been picked.

15 SENTENCE TYPES

A Look at these sentences.

1 Sekhar worked hard.
2 He won a scholarship.

Each sentence has a subject and *one verb* in the predicate part. Such sentences are called **simple sentences**.

B Look at this sentence:

Sekhar worked hard and passed in the first division.

This sentence has two different clauses of the same grammatical class linked together. The clauses are:

Sekhar worked hard.
He passed in the first division.

They are linked by the conjunction *and.* They are called principal clauses or main clauses.

The conjunctions that are used to link main clauses are called 'co-ordinating conjunctions' or 'co-ordinators'.

Sentences in which two or more main clauses are linked by co-ordinating conjunctions are called **compound sentences**.

Here is a list of co-ordinating conjunctions with examples of the compound sentences they form.

or:	You may go home or read in the library.
Either .... or :	You may either stay in the hostel or stay with a relative of yours.
Neither .... nor :	The old woman could neither read nor write.
but :	I went to his house several times, but I was unable to meet him.
yet :	He is very rich, yet he is not happy.
still :	The best doctors are attending on him, still he is not out of danger.
for :	I am very tired, for I have been working all day.
so :	There was no quorum, so the meeting was adjourned.
not only ... but also :	The enemy not only captured the city, but also destroyed several factories and buildings.
therefore :	He was absent without leave for several days, therefore his name was removed from the rolls.

nevertheless : He had a first-class, nevertheless he was unable to get admission in the college.

Exercise 1

Combine each of the following groups of sentences into a compound sentence using one or more of the co-ordinating conjunctions.

1 He is honest. He is faithful.
2 He knocked. No one came to open the door.
3 He gave us a long passage. He asked us to write a precis of it.
4 He gave us a nice dinner. He also drove us back home.
5 I lost my way. I asked a policeman to help me. He could not, being new to the place himself.
6 The guide took us round the fort. He gave us a lot of information. We didn't have the time to see everything.
7 His marks were not high. He managed to get admission in that college.
8 The time was short. He completed the work.

Exercise 2

Change the following simple sentences into compound sentences:

Example:

Simple sentence: To his great disappointment he failed in the examination.

Compound sentence: He failed in the examination and was greatly disappointed.

1 Owing to the failure of the monsoon, there was a severe drought.
3 On account of mismanagement the company suffered a great loss.
3 Threatening the traveller with a knife, the thief robbed him of all his money.
4 Being thoroughly prepared, he answered all the questions very well.
5 You have the choice of coming with me to Bombay or going to your uncle's place in Madras.
6 Standing on the top of a hill, the General watched the fighting.
7 We had not completed the work even by six o'clock.
8 In spite of being supplied with the best weapons the army could not win the battle.

C Sentences which have a main clause and a subordinate clause are called **complex sentences**. A complex sentence can have more subordinate clauses than one, but only one main clause.

Example:

If you have flown a kite, you will know *that it goes up in the air when you pull it against the wind*. (One main clause and three subordinate clauses.)

There are three kinds of subordinate clauses: (1) the adjectival clause, (2) the adverbial clause and (3) the noun clause.

Adjectival or Relative Clauses

Look at these sentences:

The young man *who was here a little while ago* is the President of the Students' Union.

His eye caught a heap of letters *which were lying on the table*.

The clause in italics in each sentence does the work of an adjective.

Who is used to refer to persons, *which* to things, animals, etc. and *that* to persons as well as things.

When the adjectival clause defines a place, time or reason, we use *where, when* and *why* in place of the relative pronoun.

Example:

We visited the house where Mahatma Gandhi was born. (place)

At a time when prices are high, we must minimise our expenditure. (time)

Could you tell me the reason why he has resigned? (reason)

The possessive form *whose* can also introduce a relative clause.

Example: Here is the man whose house was burgled.

Exercise 3

Combine each of the following pairs of sentences, turning the italicized sentence into an adjectival clause. The first is an example.

1 *A lady composed this song*. She is visiting us today.
Answer: The lady who composed this song is visiting us today.
2 *You took some books from me*. Have you read them?
3 I bought a watch. *It shows the date*.
4 *A thief broke into my neighbour's house*. He has been caught.
5 *You borrowed a dictionary from me last week*. Would you please return it?
6 *A man used to come here every day to beg*. He was found to have Rs. 5,000 in the bank!
7 *You suspect the man*. The police find no reason to suspect him.

8 This is Mr Chowdhury, the great artist. *One of his pictures was sold recently for Rs. 10,000.* (Use: one of whose.)
9 *You sent me a boy yesterday*. I am impressed with him.
10 *You sent me some books*. I found them very informative.
11 The man was the first principal of this college. *His portrait adorns the library*.
12 The grammar book has been sold out. *He wrote it*.

Exercise 4

Look at these sentences:

A friend of mine is coming to see me today.
I worked with him in the secretariat.

We can combine these sentences as follows:

A friend of mine with whom I worked in the secretariat is coming to see me today.

(Note that *him* has been changed into the relative pronoun *whom* and the preposition *with* is placed before this relative pronoun.)

Combine each of the following pairs of sentences, turning the second sentence into an adjectival clause, as shown above.

1 I walked towards a bench in the park.
Some boys were sitting on it.
2 The thief carried away the box.
We had kept our clothes in it.
3 The officer cancelled the licence of the ration shop.
There were several complaints against it.
4 In the front hall of the office you will see a receptionist.
You can get the information from her.
5 The boys climbed a tree.
They were able to watch the match from there.
6 He gave me a book.
There were some very interesting stories in it.
7 He introduced me to a person.
I was able to contact the Minister through him.
8 He gave me a key.
I opened my box with it.

Look at this sentence:

I want to buy a watch which will show the day and the date.

In this sentence, the adjectival clause answers the question: 'which (or what kind of) watch?' This type of clause is called a defining adjectival clause.

Now look at this sentence:

Raju has gone to stay with his father, *who is now in Delhi*.

In this sentence the adjectival clause (in italics) adds some information about the noun that it refers to, but does not define it.

An adjectival clause of this kind is called 'a non-defining' adjectival clause.

A comma separates this clause.

Exercise 5

Combine each of the following pairs of sentences, turning the sentence in italics into an adjectival clause, separating the clause by a comma or commas where this is necessary.

1 Cricket is played in several countries. *It is called the king of games.*
2 *Mihir Sen was the first man to swim the Palk Straits.*
He was born in Purulia in West Bengal.
3 My uncle sent me a lovely birthday present.
He likes me very much.
4 Saturday is named after Saturn.
It is the last day of the week.
5 Mrs Rao introduced me to her husband.
I had not seen him before.

Adverbial Clauses

1 *Adverbial clause of Time*

Examples:

(1) *Main clause*	(2) *Conjunction*	(3) *Adverbial clause*
I found the house locked	when	I reached home.
Wait here	till/until	I come back.
The train had left	before	we reached the station.
He hasn't written to us	since	he left home.

In the sentences in the table, the adverb clauses come after the main clause. They can also come before the main clause in several cases: e.g.

When I reached home, I found the house locked.

2 *Adverbial Clause of Place*

Examples:

(1) *Main clause*	(2) *Conjunction*	(3) *Adverbial Clause*
Put these keys	where	we can find them easily.
You may go	wherever	you like.

3 *Adverbial clause of Purpose*

Examples:

The police officer went out in plain clothes so that no one might recognize him.

In place of *so that* we can also use *in order that* or simply *that*:

The police officer went out in plain clothes in order that no one might recognize him.
Speak more loudly that he may hear you.

4 *Adverbial Clause of Reason or Cause*

Examples:

(1) *Main Clause*	(2) *Conjunction*	(3) *Adverbial Clause*
He will win the election	because	he is very popular.
I believe the story	since	it comes from you.
I didn't attend office	as	I was not well.

5 *Adverbial Clause of Result or Effect*

Examples:

(1) *Main Clause*	(2) *Conjunctions*	(3) *Adverbial Clause*
Our soldiers fought so bravely	that	the enemy suffered a crushing defeat.
It rained very heavily for two days	so that	the rivers were in spate.

He was so weak he could not even sit up in bed. (The conjunction *that* is understood.)

Exercise 6

Combine each of the following pairs of sentences using *so.... that*.

1 He was very nervous.
He forgot what he had wanted to say.
2 The box was very heavy.
I had to get a porter to carry it.
3 The compartment was very crowded.
We could not find a seat.
4 His offence was very serious.
The judge wanted to give him a deterrent punishment.
5 He had prepared very well for the examination.
He was able to answer all the questions correctly.

Exercise 7

Combine each of the following pairs of sentences using *such .... that*. The first one is done for you as an example.

1 He used very bad words.
I don't like to repeat them.
Answer: He used such bad words that I don't like to repeat them.
2 The boy has very fine manners.
Everyone likes him very much.
3 I had had a very heavy lunch.
I didn't want my tea.
4 Our soldiers fought with great courage.
The enemy suffered a crushing defeat.
5 He speaks with great eloquence.
He can get anyone to his side.

6 *Adverbial Clause of Condition*

Example:

If you take exercise regularly, you will keep fit and healthy.

The adverbial clause can also express a negative condition.

If you don't come in time, you will be marked absent.

Unless you take exercise daily, you will not keep fit

Look at these sentences:

Take an umbrella with you, in case it rains.

I took down his telephone number, in case I had to speak to him again.

We generally use *in case* to introduce a condition or eventuality, when the main clause refers to the action to be taken to meet that condition or eventuality.

Exercise 8

Combine each of the following pairs of sentences into a complex sentence, turning the first sentence into an adverbial clause with an appropriate conjunction: *if, in case*.

1 Get one hundred marks.
Then you will get a prize. (if)
2 Cut down your expenses.
Then you can save something. (if)
3 Read a large number of books.
Then you can improve your English. (if)
4 'Take another step.
You are a dead man.' (if)
5 Are you likely to go to the post office?
Then please post these letters for me. (in case)
6 Electricity may fail.
So keep a few candles at hand. (in case)

Exercise 9

Rewrite the following sentences using *unless* in place of *if*.

1 If you don't go in your uniform, you will not be admitted into the grounds.
2 How can I attend the function if I am not invited?
3 If there is no quorum, we cannot hold the meeting.
4 You are likely to be punished, if you don't express your regret.
5 Our petition will not be considered if all of us do not sign it.

Hypothetical or Imagined Condition

The adverb clauses of condition illustrated above express conditions which may or may not be fulfilled.

Look at this sentence:

If I had a lot of money, I would build a house and buy a car.

The condition here is generally not one that is expected to be fulfilled.

(Note that the verb in an *if*-clause of this kind is in the simple past tense and the verb phrase in the main clause is *should/would/could/might* + verb).

Here is another example.

If he changed his views, we would elect him. (But he won't change his views.)

The *if*-clause can also be used to express a purely imagined and untrue condition.

If Raju were here, he would support me. (But he is not here.)
If I were you, I wouldn't put up with this insult. (But I am not you.)

(Note the use of *were* in such clauses, and also the past tense form of the verb in the main clause.)

Exercise 10

Supply the correct tense forms of the verbs given in brackets.

1 If he (agree), we shall elect him as our president.
2 Take my advice. If you do so, everything (go off) well.
3 I don't know how to operate this machine. If I (know) it, I would show you how to do it.
4 I am not hungry. If you (be) hungry you may eat.
5 If I (be) you, I would not undertake the journey in the present circumstances.
6 If Gandhiji (be) alive, he (be) unhappy to see the violence in the country.
7 If you got a lakh of rupees in a lottery, tell me what you (do).
8 If he (eat) more, he will be sick.

Unfulfilled Condition in the Past

Look at these sentences:

If he hadn't wasted his time, he would have passed.
If he had asked me, I would have helped him.

The adverbial clauses in these sentences express an unfulfilled condition relating to the past. Note the use of the past perfect tense in the clause, and the use of *would have + past participle* in the main clause.

Exercise 11

Rewrite the following sentences putting the verb in brackets in the correct tense.

1 If he (work) hard, he could certainly have passed.
2 If you had come a little earlier, you (get) a ticket.
3 If the fire engines (arrive) an hour earlier, the building could have been saved.
4 If he (be) more alert, he could have avoided the accident.
5 If he (strictly follow) the doctor's instructions, he would not have had a relapse.
6 If I had known you were coming, I (met) you at the station.

7 *Adverbial Clause of Concession*

a Look at this sentence:
Although he was ill, he attended to his office work.

Here the clause in italics expresses a concession. It admits a fact: he was ill.

Clauses of this kind are called *adverbial clauses of concession*. The sentence can be written with *but, still* or *yet*.

He was ill, but/still/yet he attended to his office work.

8 *Adverbial Clause of Manner*

a Look at these sentences:
Do *as I tell you*.
Plants breathe *as animals do*.

The clauses in italics are called *adverbial clauses of manner*. They express the manner in which the action expressed by the verb in the main clause is done or is to be done.

b Look at this sentence:
He speaks *as if he knew everything under the sun*.

The clause means: as he would speak if he knew everything under the sun. (which is not the case)

We can also use *as though* in place of *as if*, in such sentences.

Exercise 12

Express the idea in each pair of sentences below in one sentence using *as if* or *as though*.

Example:

He screamed in great fear.
One might think he had seen a ghost.
Answer: He screamed in great fear as if he had seen a ghost.

1 He started ordering all the servants in the house.
One might think he was the master of the house. (But he wasn't)
2 He spoke to us discourteously.
One might think we had gone to him to beg. (But we hadn't gone to him to do so.)
3 He described the shooting of the bison very vividly.
One might think he saw it himself. (But he hadn't seen it.)
4 He walked with unsteady steps.
One might think he was drunk. (But he wasn't.)
5 Look at the way that man walks.
One might think he is the monarch of all he surveys. (But of course he isn't.)

9 *Adverbial Clause of Comparison*

Look at these sentences:

He is not so stupid *as he looks*.
He speaks much better *than he writes*.

The clauses in italics are *adverbial clauses of comparison*. They are introduced by *as* or *than*. *As* is used when the adjective or adverb in the main clause is in the positive degree. *Than* is used when it is in the comparative degree.

Exercise 13

Look at these sentences:

The red sari costs Rs. 250.
The blue sari costs Rs. 300.

We can compare the cost of the saris and say:

The red sari is not as expensive as the blue sari.
The red sari is less expensive than the blue sari.
The blue sari is more expensive than the red sari.

Write three sentences as shown above, for each of the following pairs of sentences. Use the adjective or adverb given in the brackets.

1 The one-room house costs Rs. 20,000.
The two-room house costs Rs. 30,000. (expensive)
2 The bedroom is twelve by twelve.
The drawing room is fourteen by fourteen. (big)
3 The blue box weighs ten kilos.
The red box weighs fifteen kilos. (heavy)
4 The market road is twenty feet wide.
The hospital road is thirty feet wide. (wide)
5 My watch gains five minutes a day.
Your watch gains seven minutes a day. (fast)

The Noun Clause

The teacher told me *that I was wrong*. (functions as object of the verb *told*)

That he will be appointed is certain. (subject of verb *is*)

Our hope is *that he will improve*. (subject complement)

We were certain *that he would pass*. (complement of the adjective *certain*)

The belief *that stars have some influence on our lives* is still common.

(The noun clause in italics is in apposition to the noun *belief*.)

Wh-clauses as Noun Clauses

Wh-clauses do all the functions of *that* clauses. But in addition to these, they can function as objects of prepositions.

Examples:

Subject: What you say is true.

Object: I don't know what he would say to this idea.

Subject Complement: The question is who will bell the cat.

In apposition: My question, who is responsible for the loss, has not been answered.

Adjectival Complement: I wasn't sure whose mistake it was.

Object of Preposition: He is against whatever I want to do.

If / whether clauses as noun clauses

I asked him if/whether he can speak French.

Whether he comes or not doesn't worry me.

(Note that in some cases both *if* and *whether* can be used, but in some only *if* and in others only *whether*.)

Exercise 14

Rewrite each of the following bits of conversation in indirect speech.

1 Ashok: Did you finish reading the book I gave you? (Ashok asked Mohan if.....)
Mohan: Not yet, Ashok. (Mohan said...)
2 Ashok: Will you return it next week?
Mohan: I shall.
3 Leela: Where did you buy these bangles?
Kamala: I bought them in Hyderabad.
4 Leela: What stones are there on these bangles?
Kamala: They are a kind of imitation diamond. You get them at some shops in Charminar, Hyderabad.

Exercise 15

Rewrite each of the following pairs of sentences as one sentence with a noun clause functioning as a complement.

1 He may have lost his way.
That is my fear.
2 She hasn't got the money.
That is the fact.
3 The earth was flat.
This was the belief in very old times.
4 This year the harvest should be quite good.
That is our expectation.
5 We should drop the plan.
That is my suggestion.

Exercise 16

Combine each of the following pairs of sentences into one sentence with a noun clause functioning as a complement of an adjective.

1 He will be completely cured.
The doctor is hopeful.
2 The bridge will give way.
The engineers are afraid.
3 The management will concede our demands.
We can be certain.

4 The prices will go down hereafter.
You can be sure.

5 He will pass.
I am confident.

Exercise 17

Combine each of the following pairs of sentences into one sentence turning the first sentence into a noun clause as object of a preposition.

1 You have something.
Try to manage with it.

2 The radio announcement said something yesterday about licences.
Did you listen to it?

3 They have suggested something.
I am against it.

4 There are things that you cannot have.
Don't long for them.

5 What happened in the library?
Tell me all about it.

Exercise 18

Rewrite each of the following pairs of sentences into one sentence turning one of the sentences into a noun clause functioning as subject.

1 He said something.
It is not clear.

2 When will the elections take place?
This has not been announced.

3 Why were the appointments not made?
This is not known.

4 Who is going to organize the show?
This has not been decided.

5 Where will the tournament take place?
This is yet to be decided.

Part II

Composition

1 LETTER WRITING

Read the letter given below, carefully.

A letter to a friend you met by chance after many years.

20, Maidan Road.
Calicut.
20th August 1981.

Dear Virendra,

Thank you very much for your letter which I've just received.

You are perfectly right about my memory for names–it is vey poor indeed. But in this case I don't blame myself very much; after all, we met after about seven years and the meeting was so unexpected. In fact, it took me quite some time to realize that you always used to call me Subbu.

As soon as I got back here, I rushed into our store room and got hold of my favourite album. And once I opened it, I was back in the good old days. How I wish they could come back! What fun we had together and how happy we could be even with tests and examinations to worry us!

Well, things have changed, but it was great meeting you after so long. I know you travel a lot more than I do. So if you happen to come this way again, do make it a point to break your journey at least for a day. I shall look forward to that day.

For now all the best.

Yours sincerely,
Subramanian (Subbu!)

That was a personal letter, which one writes to friends and relations. Note its parts.

1 *The heading*

This is the writer's address and the date written at the top right hand corner. Note the order of the details in the address: number or name of the house, name of street and town or city.

The date can be written in several ways: for example, January 16th 1982 or 16th Jan., 1982.

2 *The salutation*

The forms for letters to relations usually are: My dear Father/ Mother, My dear Uncle/Aunt, My dear Brother/Sister, Dear Raju etc.

The forms for letters to friends usually are: Dear Virendra, Dear Mr Panicker, Dear Mrs Raman, Dear Miss Smith, Dear Dr. Kamath, etc.

3 *The body of the letter*

This usually has three parts: an introduction, a message (main information) and a conclusion.

A good personal letter must read true and be conversational. Secondly, make your style personal and intimate, also use contracted forms (e.g., 'you've' for 'you have').

4 *The subscription*

This is written below the body of the letter usually to the right. The forms to friends usually are: Yours sincerely, Yours very sincerely. The forms to relatives are: Yours affectionately, Your loving son/ daughter/brother etc. (Note that there is no apostrophe(') for *yours*.)

5 *The address*

Write the address neatly and legibly on the envelope. Make it clear, correct and full to help the postman deliver it to the person it is meant for.

A. Personal Letters

Here are some personal letters given as examples:

1 You hold two complimentary tickets for a variety entertainment. Write a letter to a friend of yours inviting him to accompany you.

15 University Road,
Cochin.
10th August, 1982.

My dear Murali,

Many thanks for your kind letter of 31st July. I am very sorry it has taken me long to send this reply. The day I received your letter I left for Trichur to play in the State Football Tournament. I hope you will excuse me for my long silence.

On my return from Trichur, I find two complimentary tickets for a Variety Entertainment waiting for me. The show is coming off on Sunday next and is being organized by the local Youth Club. I shall be most happy if you can come with me to the show.

Some of the city recreation clubs, and music and dance sabhas are presenting very interesting items and the show is bound to be entertaining. The highlight of the show, I am told, is a scene from Kathakali presented by the Kerala Club. I know how interested you are in this art form and I hope you will find it convenient to come. Please drop me a line in reply.

My regards to your parents.

Yours sincerely,
Prasad

2 Write a letter to a friend of yours telling her about your future plans after leaving college.

24 Station Road,
Trichur
July 28, 1982.

Dear Savithri,

Thank you very much for your kind letter of July 20th. It was such a pleasure to hear from you after a long time. I wonder how you found time to write to me in the midst of your preparation for the final examination.

You ask me what I intend to do after I take my B.Sc. degree. It has all along been my ambition to study medicine and become a doctor. But I am not sure whether I'll get a high enough rank to qualify me for admission. If I don't join a medical college, I would like to join the Library Science Course in the University. I can complete this course in a year and be sure of a job too. That would be a great relief to my father, who is to retire two years hence.

You didn't tell me what your plans are. How about going in for research in your field of study?

With kind regards,

Yours sincerely,
Seethalakshmy

Learn how personal letters are begun and concluded. Here are a few ways of beginning them.

(Many) thanks for your kind letter dated ....
It is a long time since I heard from you.
This letter may perhaps come as a surprise to you.

Here are a few ways in which you can conclude your letters:

With kind regards,
With warm and affectionate regards,
With love,

Exercises

A Write a letter:

1 to your cousin/friend who is in another town inviting him to spend the Diwali holidays with you and your family.

2 to a friend thanking him for the hospitality extended to you during the holidays.

3 to your father telling him about the career you would like to choose after graduation, and why.

4 to your mother telling her about your progress at college.

5 to your father's friend who forgot his umbrella in your house. Say you will have it sent to him on Sunday.

6 to your cousin telling him about the new bicycle you have bought and why you like it.

B

1 You had a minor accident while riding a bicycle. You received a very anxious letter of enquiry from your father. Write a letter to him about the accident asking him not to worry.

2 Your neighbour left the town, locking up his house. A thief broke into the house but you noticed this in time and the thief ran away. Write a letter informing your neighbour of this incident.

B Professional and Business Letters

Read this letter carefully.

A letter to the editor of the local daily complaining about the neglect of the roads and drains in your locality.

16 Mahatma Gandhi Road,
Bangalore,
Karnataka.

20.9.1982.

To

The Editor,
The Deccan Herald,
Bangalore.

Sir,

I would like to bring to the notice of everyone who values cleanliness something extremely worrying about our locality. All the roads in our area have remained unswept for at least two weeks, with the result that all of us have to suffer an ever-growing foul smell. All the by-lanes are full of stagnant water since most drains stopped working weeks ago. The result is millions of mosquitoes and flies. Our only park which used to be a sight for sore eyes will soon become an eyesore; no one pays any attention to it.

Sir, many of us believe that it will soon be too late to save the situation. Will the authorities wake up to it?

Yours truly,
V.M.Kutty

The letter above belongs to a second category of letters, called professional, business or official letters. Such letters are written to a company, or a person holding some official position.

In this category of letters are included letters to editors of newspapers, applications for jobs, applications for leave of absence, representations and petitions to authorities such as chairmen of municipalities, presidents of panchayat boards, the postal department, the police department, etc.

Study the parts of this type of letter:

1 *The heading* written at the top right-hand corner. To the left and little below the level of the date, write the designation (Manager, Chairman, President, Inspector of Police, the Post-Master, etc.) of the person you are writing to together with the address of the company, business concern, office, etc.

2 *The salutation*: To companies, business houses, etc.:
Dear Sir, Dear Sirs, Gentlemen.
To officials:
Sir, Dear Sir, Madam.

To persons in official or business positions when they are addressed by name: Dear Mr. Mathur, Dear Mrs Francis, Dear Miss Sakuntala.

3 *The body* usually consists of three parts: reference or introduction, information and conclusion.

4 *Subscription*: for example, business houses, etc.:

Yours faithfully, Yours truly.

For person addressed as Mr _____, Mrs _____, Shri _____, etc.
Yours sincerely, Yours very sincerely,
Editor of newspaper: Yours truly,
Headmaster, Principal: Yours obediently.

5 *The address*

Write the address clearly on the envelope giving details of district, state, country, etc. wherever necessary.

Here are some specimens of professional and business letters:

1 You ordered some books from a bookseller and on opening the parcel found some of the books damaged and two missing. Write a letter to the bookseller asking for replacement of the damaged books and the despatch of the missing ones.

40 Krishna Menon Road,
Trivandrum,
1st September 1982.

To

The Manager,
India Book Stall,
Fort, Bombay.

Dear Sir,

The books that I ordered on 15th August arrived yesterday. Many thanks for the prompt execution of my order.

I regret, however, to inform you that when the parcel was opened three of the books I ordered were found to be badly damaged and unfit for use. I attach a list of these books.

Secondly, the following books were not in the parcel:

1 Complete Works of Shakespeare: Globe Edition.
2 David Copperfield: Charles Dickens.

I request you to replace the three damaged books and also to send the two missing books. I shall arrange to return the damaged books on hearing from you.

Yours faithfully,
Pramila George

Enclosed: List of damaged books.

2 Write an application for the post of a typist-clerk in response to an advertisement in the newspapers.

12/K Sanjay Nagar,
Bombay.
1st August 1982.

To

The Manager,
The Co-operative Urban Bank Ltd.,
Jawaharnagar,
Kozhikode.

Sir,

This refers to your advertisement in *The Hindu* of 25.7.1982 for two posts of typist-clerks in your bank. I submit this application for one of the posts.

I have passed the Intermediate Examination of the Board of Intermediate Education, Kerala obtaining a first class. While studying in the Intermediate Course, I learnt typewriting too and passed the Higher Grade Examination held last April. I can type 50 words per minute.

I am at present working in a pharmaceutical firm in a temporary capacity and the management has agreed to relieve me at a week's notice, in case I wish to leave.

I am aged 19 years and possess good health.

I enclose two testimonials, one from my Principal and the other from the local Magistrate.

If I am appointed, I shall do my best to give you complete satisfaction in my work.

Yours faithfully,
V.S. Raghavan

Exercises

1 Write a letter to the Manager, R.T.O., complaining about the bad behaviour of a bus conductor.
2 Write a letter to the Director of Public Instruction requesting him to preside over the College Day celebrations. (You are the President of the College Union).
3 Write a letter to a dealer in sports goods ordering half a dozen cricket bats and balls.
4 Write a letter to the Manager, Regal Hotel in Madras, asking for a single room for you for three days.
5 The walls in your town are frequently disfigured by the sticking of ugly posters. Write a letter to the police authorities expressing your disapproval and giving helpful suggestions.
6 An important man in your town, known for his philanthropy, has passed away. Write a letter to the Editor of a newspaper praising his services to the community and suggesting a suitable memorial for him.
7 'Wanted: A library assistant for the Municipal Central Library. Apply to the Commissioner, Calicut Municipality.' Write an application in response to this advertisement.

C Social Letters

These include invitations (also acceptance or inability to accept an invitation), letters of congratulation or condolence, and letters to thank someone for presents, favours done, etc.

Social letters can be formal or informal, depending on the person we address or the occasion for writing the letter. Generally the formal ones are written in the third person and the informal ones, in the first person. Study the specimens given below:

1 A formal invitation and its acceptance.
Invitation:

Sri Ismail Seth

and

Mrs Farida Seth

request the pleasure of Dr. and Mrs. Sultan Ali's
company at buffet lunch
on Monday, 17th January, 1983, at 1 p.m.

RSVP 24 Rajaji Road,
Trivandrum.
Tel: 82453

Acceptance:

Dr and Mrs. Sultan Ali have pleasure in accepting Ismail Seth and Mrs Farida Seth's invitation to lunch at 1 p.m. on 17th January 1983.

23/11, Gandhi Marg,
Trivandrum.

2 An informal invitation

10 Ashok Nagar,
Calicut.
March 30, 1983.

Dear Dr Rajan,

Shobha and I would feel delighted if Mrs Rajan and you would join us at dinner on Friday 2nd April 1983 at 8 p.m. I am sorry for giving such short notice but hope you can come.

Warm regards.

Yours sincerely,
K.V. Raman

Refusal

21 Sarojini Devi Road,
Calicut.
April 1, 1983.

Dear Shri Raman,

I have just received your kind invitation to dinner, for which many thanks. We would have accepted it gladly but unfortunately Radha has a bad cold and I have to be away in Cochin for the week-end. So neither of us can join you and we regret it. Radha joins me in sending our warm regards to your wife and your mother.

Yours sincerely,
S.K. Rajan

Exercises

1 Write a letter to your class teacher inviting him to lunch on your birthday.

2 You are the President of the Students' Union. The Union has decided to give a party to a retiring professor.
Prepare a formal invitation from you and the Students' Union to the members of the staff to attend the party.

3 Write a letter of congratulations to a student of your college who has won the first prize in an inter-collegiate elocution competition.

2 EXPANSION

Here you are generally given a well-known saying, a proverb, a maxim or a quotation. Such sayings, etc. are packed with meaning. Here are some examples.

A stitch in time saves nine.
Rome was not built in a day.
The early bird catches the worm.
Penny wise, pound foolish.

You are required to expand the statement, giving its full meaning and significance. You can also cite examples or illustrations to support the statement. Your final product should be a closely-knit piece of writing—a complete piece of composition.

Here are some helpful directions for doing this exercise.

Think over the meaning, significance and implications of the statement given to you.
Write down the important points in the right order.

3 Think of one or two illustrations if possible to support the main idea.
4 Put your thoughts in simple language, linking them appropriately. If a limit has been set, do not exceed it.
5 Avoid beginning with sentences such as the following: This statement means ....
The meaning of the proverb is ....
This is a well-known proverb ....
6 Carefully revise what you have written.

Study the following examples.

1 *Make Hay while the Sun Shines.*

Main points:
a explanation
b uncertainties of life
c opportunities seldom come
d illustration
e conclusion.

It is common knowledge that farmers have to depend on the weather for their operations. For instance they have to wait for bright sunshine to dry the hay after harvest; and if they miss it, the hay will be ruined by exposure to mist or rain.

All of us are in the same position as the farmer. Life is as uncertain as the weather. There are several unpredictable factors in life. No one can predict when death will snatch it away. Health, wealth, help, co-operation of friends and relatives are all uncertain factors. Opportunities for education, employment, progress, etc. are also unpredictable. That man is, therefore, wise who seizes a situation, an opportunity, etc. when it comes along and makes the fullest use of it, to achieve his ends in life. He will fail in life if he is not vigilant and lets slip these opportunities.

We see these days a number of young persons in schools and colleges frittering away their energies and wasting their time on things other than their studies. They let slip their opportunities in their formative years and later may repent for their folly.

It is, therefore, necessary that we seize opportunities when they come to us and use them to the best advantage.

2 *A Stitch in Time Saves Nine.*

Very often an article of dress or a piece of cloth gets a little torn, but with just a stitch or two done without delay we can mend the tear. But if we postpone doing this, the tear will become larger and we may have to put in a number of stitches to mend it, or worse still, it may not be possible to mend it at all, and the article gets useless.

What is true of a piece of cloth is true of several situations of life. A damage to an article of daily use, a piece of furniture, a building, etc., can be repaired with just a little effort and expense if attended to promptly, but if neglected, the repair will entail much effort and expenditure.

The statement is very pertinent in regard to a person's health. If he has a minor ailment it can be easily cured with just a visit to the doctor, but if neglected, it may develop into serious trouble requiring prolonged treatment and numerous visits to the doctor.

Bad habits such as smoking are to be 'nipped in the bud' or they will get beyond correction or control.

Any damage, therefore, to property, health, etc. should be attended to immediately after it is detected.

3 *Sweet are the uses of Adversity*

Man as a rule longs for a life of peace and happiness. He dreads all sorrows, misfortunes and calamities such as failures in examinations, loss of money, deaths in the family and suffering from disease. Life should be for him a continuous flow of success, peace and prosperity.

But man does not realize that adversity has its own advantages. It is during moments of great stress, suffering and misfortune that the best faculties in man have shown forth. It is during such times that he turns contemplative and philosophical and becomes a believer in divine forces. When Kunti, the mother of the Pandava princes, was asked by Krishna to choose a boon, she promptly asked for a life of adversity, which alone would fix her mind on God. Long ago there was a great Sanskrit scholar who, afflicted with a serious attack of paralysis, sought the grace of the Lord and composed over a thousand masterly verses in His glory. Instances can be multiplied to prove that great things have been achieved by man in times of suffering and adversity.

Exercises

1 A rolling stone gathers no moss.
2 All that glitters is not gold.
3 A bird in the hand is worth two in the bush.
4 Too many cooks spoil the broth.
5 People who live in glass houses should not throw stones.

6 God helps those who help themselves.
7 Penny wise, pound foolish.
8 The early bird catches the worm.
9 Variety is the spice of life.
10 Slow and steady wins the race.
11 Little strokes fell great oaks.
12 The path of duty is the way to glory.
13 Beggars cannot be choosers.
14 Do unto others as you wish them to do unto you.
15 Charity begins at home.
16 It is never too late to mend.
17 An empty vessel makes the greater noise.
18 Necessity is the mother of invention.
19 Failures are stepping stones to success.
20 Birds of a feather flock together.

3 PRECIS-WRITING

A precis is a summary or a restatement of the essential ideas in a piece of writing. Another word for *precis* is the Greek word *epitome*, 'to cut upon'.

Characteristics of a good Precis

1 In a good precis, the ideas are organized and expressed in a logical sequence, so that it reads as an original piece of composition.
2 A good precis should contain all the essential ideas in the original, omitting non-essential ideas, examples, etc.
3 The language of a precis should be clear, brief and precise.
4 A good precis should be in your own words.
5 It should not much exceed or fall much short of the length prescribed. Usually the limit set is a third of the original.
6 Direct speech should, as a rule, be changed into indirect speech.

Steps for the writing of a Precis

1 Read and re-read the given passage carefully until you understand it as a whole and grasp its central idea.
2 Write down the main ideas or points of the passage leaving out unimportant or incidental details.
3 Write down a preliminary draft, having in mind the number of words prescribed. You should try to condense by remodelling the sentences of the text. Do not put in any fresh ideas.
4 Rewrite your draft. Check whether you have put in all the main ideas. Check the number of words in the final draft and bring it to the limit prescribed. Correct the mistakes, if any.
5 Write out the fair copy under the heading you have chosen.

Example:

In spite of rigorous precautions against accidents, many people are injured every year in factories and elsewhere. In addition, some people are born with physical disabilities. They are either blind or deaf or in some way deformed from birth. Up to quite recent times, little planned action was taken to fit handicapped people for employment. A number of charitable organizations tried to help them in cases of hardship; but few seriously held the idea that these people might still have abilities in other directions.

Only during the last few decades has society slowly come to acknowledge its responsibilities and to recognize that handicapped people can be trained to play a useful part in economic as well as social life. The Second World War gave importance to this. During the 1939-45 war, pressure on resources of labour compelled all fighting nations to call on the services of handicapped people for tasks adapted to, and within the limits of their capacities. A man might have lost the use of his legs, but still be able to use his hands with skill. Another person might have lost his sight, but still be capable of training in ways in which his other senses could be employed effectively in furtherance of the war effort.

In recent years, scientific inventions and discoveries have lessened the disabilities of deafness, some forms of paralysis, and other physical handicaps. Scientists working in association with engineers have devised methods by which handicapped people can take up work again.

thanks to the invention of mechanical limbs, the improvement of hearing aids and so on. (263 words)

From *Man in our Modern World*
Odhams Press Ltd., London (Adapted)

The Main Points

1 Many people in the world suffer from physical disabilities.
2 Charitable organizations help them, but do not utilize the abilities they may have.
3 Efforts in the last few decades to provide employment for the handicaped people.
4 Scientific inventions have come to the aid of the handicapped in several ways.

First Draft

Many people suffer from physical handicaps such as loss of limb, blindness or deafness caused by accidents or existing at birth. Till recent times, there have been several organizations engaged in helping them and lessening their suffering, but no thought has been given by these organizations to employing them and utilizing the abilities that they may still have. During the last few decades, especially during World War II when labour was scarce, ways and means came to be devised of discovering and appropriately utilizing the abilities that the handicapped may still have, and making them useful members of society. Scientists in collaboration with engineers have also developed instruments such as mechanical limbs and hearing aids to lessen the suffering of the handicapped and increasing their working efficiency.
(132 words)

Final Draft

Many people suffer from physical handicaps such as loss of limb, blindness or deafness. Till recently, there have been organizations engaged in lessening their suffering, but no thought has been given to utilizing the abilities that they may still have, and making them useful members of society. During the last few decades, especially during World War II, ways and means came to be devised of utilizing their abilities. Scientists and engineers have also invented instruments to lessen the suffering of the handicapped and increasing their efficiency.
(86 words)

Here are some phrases and sentences deleted in the final draft either because they are details or because they are only examples illustrating a point or idea.

.... In spite of rigorous precautions against accidents ....
.... In addition, some people are born with physical disabilities ....
.... In cases of hardship ....
.... A man might have ....
.... with skill.
Another person might have ....
.... the war effort ....
.... Some forms of paralysis ....

Secondly, note how the first three sentences of the second paragraph have been remodelled and condensed.

Suggested title

Rehabilitation of the Handicapped.

Write a precis of each of the following passages in about one third of its length, and suggest a suitable heading for it.

1 In every country people imagine that they are the best and the cleverest and the others are not so good as they are. The Englishman thinks that he and his country are the best; the Frenchman is very proud of France and everything French; the Germans and Italians think no end of their countries and many Indians imagine that India is in many ways the greatest country in the world. This is all conceit. Everybody wants to think well of himself and his country. But really there is no person who has not got some good in him and some bad. And in the same way there is no country which is not partly good and partly bad. We must take the good wherever we find it and try to remove the bad wherever it may be. We are of course most concerned with our country, India. Unhappily it is in a bad way today and most of our people are very poor and miserable. They have no pleasure in their lives. We have to find out how we can make them happier. We have to see what is good in our ways and customs and try to keep it, and whatever is bad we have to throw away. If we find anything good in other countries, we should certainly take it.

–Jawaharlal Nehru; from *Autobiography*
Messrs John Lane, The Bodley Head, Ltd.

2 There are hundreds of superstitions which survive in various parts of the country, and the study of them is rather amusing. We are told, for example, that it is unlucky to point to the new moon or to look at it through glass, but if we bow nine times to it we shall have a lucky month!

Nearly all superstitions are concerned with 'luck'. Good luck is associated with black cats, horseshoes, the finding of a pin, the threepenny bit in the Christmas pudding, the old shoe flung at a wedding party, and the dark man who is the first to step over the door-step on New Year's Day. Ill luck is associated with the howling of dogs, the spilling of salt, the crossing of knives, sitting down thirteen to a table, meeting a cross-eyed woman, walking under a ladder, the falling of a picture from the wall, the breaking of a mirror, and scores of other things.

When the fire is reluctant to burn, a servant-girl will often place a poker upright before the bars. She does not know why she does it. She has seen her mother and grandmother do it. But centuries ago a sulky fire was attributed to witchcraft, and the upright poker against the bars (which made the sign of the cross) was thought to have power to destroy the evil spell.

Now suppose you tell a scientist that you believe a certain superstition–let us say, that the howling of a dog is a sign of death. The scientist will immediately require evidence before he can accept your belief. He will want figures to prove it. It will be useless to quote two or three cases; he will want hundreds. He will want also to know (a) if it ever happens that the howling of dogs is not followed by a death, (b) if every person's death is predicted by the howling of dogs. The answer to the former question is in the affirmative, and to the latter in the negative. Your superstition will not bear investigation. It may impress an ignorant person, but it cannot face the light of facts. Your case would not carry conviction in a court of law.

Apart from this process of testing by results, however, any intelligent man will want to know the 'reason why'. What connection can there be between a howling dog and an approaching death? Can it be cause and effect? Can it be that the dog has a gift of foreseeing such events? Or is the dog the instrument employed by some uncanny power that moves invisibly in our midst?

3 It had long been suspected that there was some connection between the abundance of mosquitoes and the occurrence of malaria, since both were at their worst in the same regions and at the same seasons,

but what the connection was had not been understood. Sir Patrick Manson, reasoning from the state of things discovered by him in another disease happily unknown to us in this country, made the suggestion that the parasite might be conveyed into the human body by the mosquito in the act of biting.

Following this suggestion, Major Ronald Ross made a set of experiments in India by feeding all the different kinds of mosquito procurable on the blood of malaria patients, and then dissecting and examining every part of their bodies to see if there was any trace of the parasite. Hundreds of mosquitoes were thus laboriously examined, but for two years there was no result. Still the tireless investigator persevered and finally he found a species the blood of which showed certain characters in common with the blood of the malaria patients. He was soon able to prove that all the mosquitoes of that particular kind fed on the blood of malaria patients became infected with the parasite which causes the fever.

The life-history of the parasite is difficult to follow, but it is sufficient for us to understand the general results gained so far. Malarial fever in man is due to a very minute parasite living in the blood. This parasite may go on living and multiplying in the blood of man for an indefinite time, unless it is killed by drugs, but it does not go through any further stage of its life-history, and cannot infect other human beings.

A mosquito biting an infected person receives some of the parasites into its own blood; there they go through a further stage of development, and finally, the infected mosquito passes on the fully developed parasites to the next person it bites, and these soon show symptoms of malarial fever.

But the last part of this story had still to be proved. An enthusiastic student of science, who had not been in a malarious country since his childhood, deliberately allowed himself to be bitten by infected mosquitoes brought to London from Rome. He took malaria, and the case was proved.

4 Slow-motion photography is often used in newsreels to show exactly how a horse jumped or a sportsman played a stroke.

If you want to film a scene in slow motion you run the camera twice as fast as usual, which sounds ridiculous, but isn't. When a film camera is running at normal speed, it takes twenty four pictures a second. When the film is run through the film projector in the camera twenty-four pictures a second appear on the screen. This is because the camera which took the pictures and the projector which shows them run at the same speed. If you are filming in slow motion, however, the camera runs at twice the normal speed, yet in spite of this, the projector which shows the film will be run at the normal speed, and this means that the projector will show the film at half the speed at which it was photographed. On the screen everything appears at half the speed at which the camera recorded it when it was filmed. In other words, things will seem to be done in 'slow motion'.

This trick can also work the other way round. In a film comedy it sometimes looks very funny if all the characters suddenly move very fast. The director may want to tell his audience in an amusing way that life in a particular city is lived at a tremendous pace. He shows a shot of the city streets in which men and women seem to be darting about at top speed.

To get the effect you do just the opposite of what you did to get 'slow motion'. Instead of running the film camera at twice the normal speed, you run it at half the normal speed. The projector in the cinema is, as usual, run at the normal speed. This time the projector shows the film at twice the speed at which it was photographed, since the camera was run at half the normal speed.

You may find this difficult to work out at first. But the thing to remember is that a projector in the cinema always runs at the same speed, so if the action is to be slowed down, the projector must be showing things which have been taken by a camera that was moving faster than usual. If the projector is to show things speeded up, it must be showing things which have been taken by a camera whose speed was slower than usual. Either way the people who appear in the scene will have been acting at a perfectly normal pace.

4 ESSAY-WRITING

Essays may be divided into four main types:

1 Descriptive
2 Narrative
3 Expository or reflective
4 Argumentative

A. First, some general guidelines for essay-writing.

A good essay must hold the reader's attention and have the following qualities:

1 It must be based on your own thinking and experience, not on what other people say about the subject. Think your own thoughts about it and express them in your own language. But study the best models and learn from them.

2 An essay must possess unity and coherence. Unity is achieved by good planning, while for coherence we use words that help the sentences to stick together. Some useful linking words and phrases are:

a Words: and, or, but, still, however, therefore, also, yet, nevertheless, first, next, then, firstly, secondly, lastly, finally, consequently, accordingly, now, then, soon, later, meanwhile, moreover, etc.

b Phrases: on the other hand, on the contrary, in addition, in conclusion, in other words, to sum up, in brief (short), as a result, etc.

3 Every essay has its structure—a beginning, a body and a conclusion. A striking beginning can impress the reader and create interest. Here are a few possible ways in which to begin an essay:

a With a *definition* (e.g., to being an essay on 'Inflation': Inflation may be defined as rise in prices brought about by expansion of the supply of money....) and then try to illustrate it or support it with facts.

b With one or more *questions* both to provoke our reader and to prepare him for the answer that we supply in the essay. (e.g. for an essay on 'The choice of a career': What is a career? Is it merely an occupation or a profession or is it much more?).

c With an incident or experience of our own. This is often done in narrative or biographical essays. (e.g. for an essay on 'An accident I witnessed,' we may begin with: 'It was a warm Sunday afternoon last June. I was riding my new bicycle which my father had given me as a birthday present.')

d With a brief description to create the atmosphere for the main event. This will naturally vary from one type of essay to another.

The introduction is followed by the body which contains the main points—the core of the essay. The body must always be based on an outline plan.

The third and the last part of an essay is the conclusion. Like the introduction, it too varies from subject to subject.

a It provides a brief and clearly written summary of the main points of the essay.

b It often contains the most memorable event/incident of the story/description, etc.

c It occasionally draws a lesson or moral from the essay.

d It may be used to raise a related question (or questions) for the reader to think about.

Remember to conclude the essay on a suitable and striking note.

B Here now are a few hints on the types of essays.

1 A **descriptive essay** attempts to describe a place, an event or happening, a person or a natural phenomenon. A few examples are:

a Places—the Museum, the Kovalam beach.

b Natural phenomena—volcanoes, the seasons.

c Things—the helicopter, the television set, the newspaper.

d Events—a fire, an accident, a celebration.

e Persons—the author I like most, the policeman.

In a descriptive essay, there must be a central idea or impression and the details must be built around this, in an ordered way. Always remember that a good essay is an organic whole.

2 A **narrative essay** gives an orderly account of an event or happening. A few examples are: The cigarette that burnt six houses, A day without water, The inter-school tournament.

A narrative is a story, so it must be told in the order of occurrence of the incidents.

Two other things require particular attention.

a Every narrative has a main event. Show its central importance.

b A good narrative is one that succeeds in keeping the excitement of the event to the very end. The end must therefore be striking and significant.

3 **An expository or reflective essay** contains the thoughts of its author on a certain subject, usually abstract (e.g., Truth, Friendship, Honesty) or on social, political and religious and economic questions (e.g. the caste system, democracy, women's education, Hinduism).

The most important part of such an essay is a clear understanding of what is involved in the topic. You must decide on the aspect that you consider as the most important. Also make sure that you write of what you know best.

4 **An argumentative essay** is usually one through which the author tries to persuade or convince. Such essays are based on facts rather than on imagination. In them the writer argues for or against something and, in most cases, proposes a solution to a problem.

The most important part of an argumentative essay is its convincing presentation. For this you must remember the following:

a A few facts, carefully selected and well organized, can do much more than a large number of facts badly organized.

b Build your essay on proved facts.

c Lastly, since an argument is always for or against something, be fair to the opposite viewpoint.

The following are true of all forms of good writing:

a Always begin with an outline plan. To prepare it you must think of the different aspects of the topic and then note down the main points in a definite order.

b Write your essay in short paragraphs. Each paragraph must add a fresh point to your essay.

c Never spend too much time on one idea at the expense of the others.

d Your essay must show balance. For this it is important to pay attention to all the important ideas.

e It is wrong to use too many quotations in an essay.

f Avoid repetitions and be brief and clear.

g Lastly, remember your essay is a piece of personal writing. So try never to use unfamiliar words and expressions. Also, avoid the use of difficult words and involved sentences.

f Always go over your essay to make sure it does not contain any mistakes.

d *Specimen Essays*

1 **My first Day in College**

(Outline plan: The first day feeling, the atmosphere and my reaction to it; the day's events and how I felt at the end. As I now see it.)

Our college began on the first day of July. It was a wet morning when I left home to catch the bus. And as I walked towards the bus stop, my mind was full of hopes and fears.

The first hour at college passed without any notable event. We got through the admission formalities, paid the term fees, and waited for the introductory lecture.

Then something happened which shook me out of my confidence. As I was walking towards the auditorium for the principal's address, a group of boys stood in my way. They asked me a whole lot of questions and whether I answered them correctly or not, made fun of both what I said and how I said it. Then one of them, a tall and stout boy, ordered me to sing and dance. I tried to explain that I was a bad singer and had never learnt how to dance. But he had such force and authority in his voice that refusal was impossible. The senior boys who were led by this tall fellow thoroughly enjoyed making fun of my voice and movements. I felt like crying but restrained myself to save face.

This torture would have gone on for much longer but for the arrival of a lecturer who asked the boys to report at the auditorium immediately. On the way, I saw a number of other first-year boys who had suffered similar treatment. Some of them were in tears and a few others were shouting in anger and disgust.

That, however, was the worst hour of college on the first day. For, as soon as we entered the auditorium, we were given a warm and friendly reception by the Principal, the teaching staff and members of the College Union. First the Principal spoke. He told us about the facilities that would be made available to us, invited us to participate fully in the life of the college and briefly described our duties and rights as college students. The next to speak was the Union President. He apologized for the excesses of 'ragging', assured us of friendly behaviour from the seniors and invited us to join him for an afternoon's entertainment and get-together. Some other brief speeches followed his.

The meeting concluded with a sumptuous tea where the seniors made us feel at home as equals. Some of the students who had misbehaved and treated me so badly in the morning were now all smiles and friendly. A few of them apologized or explained why they had behaved as they did.

The whole afternoon was spent in outdoor games. The senior students had organized a number of matches which included a half-day cricket match, hockey and football matches and several other group games. A number of us participated in some of these and enjoyed ourselves thoroughly.

The day ended with two things. First, the Vice-Principal gave us a brief talk on the first week's time-table and co-curricular activities. Then, the Principal hosted a tea with biscuits. The day which had begun with hope and apprehension and led to fear and frustration, thus ended much better than any of us had expected. Looking back at it after several months have passed I now find that even the unpleasantness was less harmful and humiliating than I found at that time. The first day at college was a highly rewarding day in more ways than one.

2 **Women must be Equal but not Identical Partners with Men** (or Equality of Sexes, not their Identity)

(Outline plan: The need to liberate women; women's neglect costs the nation dearly. Women excel men in certain spheres of life. Essential to have equal opportunities and rewards. But there are differences; these to be accepted/acknowledged. Utilize both to maximum advantage.)

All over the world there is today a movement which seeks to liberate women. In some countries it is taking more extreme forms—processions, protests and agitations against men and our men-dominated society.

Women must be liberated in the sense that they should be enabled to play responsible roles in different walks of life. In most countries women continue to be neglected; in general there are far fewer women than men who have had the benefits of higher education or suitable careers. In some parts of the world a woman's place is still in the kitchen. Man supports the family economically, the woman serves him and looks after the children.

The neglect of one half of mankind costs the world a great deal both in economic and in social terms. A family without an educated mother is, in most cases, a poorer family than one in which everyone is educated and can earn a living. A family of the former kind may suffer in other ways too, because the mother is unable to help the children in their education and training for life. An educated and enlightened mother can make all the difference to the family fortunes. This must be equally true of nations with or without enlightened women.

In today's world we know something else which strengthens our belief in the liberation of women. It is that given equal chances and opportunities women can do as much and as well as (if not better than) the best of men. The world today has several women Prime Ministers and Presidents, a growing number of women scientists and scholars and numerous women leaders in different walks of life.

Nor need women lag behind in sport or adventure. Recently a Japanese mother and housewife conquered Mount Everest and not so long ago a woman tennis player beat a male world-class tennis champion. Women have begun to serve in the police force and the Americans are recruiting large numbers of women in their armed services.

Everything seems thus to justify the need to give equal opportunities to women. The liberation of women is essential for the liberation of mankind.

But this raises a question: should enlightened women be the same as enlightened men? This question is difficult to answer. If by equality we mean that women should do exactly what men do and avoid doing what men do not attempt, this may create more problems than it can help solve. The two sexes come to this world with different strengths and different potentialities. Each should be allowed to do what it can do best. There are professions where both men and women must play equally important roles (e.g. medicine and research). There are others where women, given equal opportunities, appear to excel men (e.g. teaching and some kinds of social service). But there are also tasks and roles which require man's physical strength rather than woman's sensibility, delicacy and quiet perseverance. It will be wrong and uneconomical to force the one to attempt the tasks that suit the other.

Equal opportunities need not mean identical training. It should mean training that provides equally rich possibilities for growth and development. For the good of mankind and our future on this earth men and women must march forward together, each contributing his/her mite to the common cause–a better and more human world.

Essay Outlines

1 *College Day*: Big event – sports and fun on all sides; inter-class matches – tea and snacks, great enthusiasm – joyful shouts; races, throws, jumps – prizes; the cultural evening – dances, songs, plays.

2 *A Flight to Delhi*: Won a prize – Rs. 3,000 or a week-end in Delhi; chose the latter; the take-off; things look small and strange from above; passed cities; rivers; jerks at one time – felt uneasy; a smooth landing. Enjoyed the flight; two hours' journey instead of two nights and one day.

3 *The Public Library*: What is it? (books, journals, magazines, a reading room); how the books are indexed (card catalogues, the decimal system); rules of the library – *x* books for *x* days, late fee, etc; the librarian – a friend and helper; the people who visit the library – different types, age groups and persons with different tastes (describe these); one of the best places to visit.

4 *Honesty*: Definitions – freedom from deceit; honesty in different aspects of life – in studies, at home, at work, etc., honesty and dishonesty in business – adulteration, black marketing, smuggling; dishonest professionals – doctors, engineers, executives, – hide income from tax inspectors, make false statements; honesty in difficult circumstances, to help the needy, to save the poor; an honest man the best example to emulate.

Essays for you to write

Narrative Essays

1 The Absent-minded Professor
2 The Day I Won my First Prize
3 How We Caught a Pickpocket
4 The Cigarette End that Destroyed a Whole Street
5 The Day of the Earthquake
6 The Unforgettable Dream

Descriptive Essays

1 When the Train Arrives at the Platform
2 Football
3 Malayalam Films
4 Examinations
5 Hobbies
6 Floods

Reflective (Expository) Essays

1 Superstitions
2 Poverty
3 Bad Manners
4 Rash Driving
5 Electricity
6 Space Exploration

Argumentative Essays

1 Village Life is Healthier than Town Life
2 Dowry is the Worst Social Evil
3 It is Bad to Feed a Snake
4 There Should be Equal Pay for Equal Work
5 'Women's Lib' is Bunkum
6 Cricket is a Better Game than Hockey
7 Everyone should Pay the Same Taxes.